LAGHU-HĀRĪTA-SMṚTI

LAGHU-HĀRĪTA-SMṚTI

(TEXT WITH ENGLISH TRANSLATION AND NOTES)

DR. SIDDHESWAR JENA
Reader -in-Sanskrit
N.C. Autonomous College, Jajpur.

BKP
BHARATIYA KALA PRAKASHAN
DELHI (INDIA)

First Published : 2004

Published by **C.P. Gautam**
BHARATIYA KALA PRAKASHAN
3421-A, IInd Floor, Narang Colony, Tri Nagar,
Delhi-110035. Phone : (O) 27393083, 30967505 (R) 27522129

ISBN : 81-8090-051-7

Laser Type Setting by
A-ONE GRAPHICS
JD-18C, IInd Floor, Pitampura, Delhi-110088
Phone : 55640278, Mob. : 9811167357

Printed by
BDH Printer at Salasar Imaging Systems
Delhi, Ph. 31045804

Dedicated

to

My revered teacher

PROFESSOR SADASHIVA PRAHARAJA

A veteran Smṛti scholar of Orissa.

Contents

Foreword

Hārīta, a celebrated ancient sage and a philosopher is also an ancient authority in the field of Dharmśāstra. The digests and commentaries on Dharmśāstra have profusely quoted *sūtras* and verses, ascribed to this great sage. Some Smṛti-texts, entitled *"Hārīta Saṁhitā"*. *"Laghu-Hārīta-Smṛti"*, and *Vṛddha-Hārīta-Smṛti* are available with his name in the printed collections of Smṛtis. Here is a small book on the *"Laghu-Hārīta-Smṛti"* edited and translated with notes by Dr. Siddheswar Jena, Reader in Sanskrit, N.C. Autonomous College, Jajpur (Orissa). He is a scholar, famous for his research in Purāṇic-studies, especially on the *Narasiṁha Purāṇa*. His three books on the *Narasiṁha Purāṇa* and one more, incorporating his articles on legends in Purāṇas have already been published.

While pursuing his research on the *Narasiṁha Purāṇa* Dr. Jena got interested in the *Laghu-Hārīta-Smṛti*, since the text of the said Purāṇa had verses, similar to those found in the said Smṛti-text. He once presented one paper on this comparative problem. Naturally, he first consulted one edition of the *Laghu-Hārīta-Smṛti*. But Mm. P.V. Kane's reference that the text contains 250 verses in the Jīvānanda edition, inspired him to make more search in the matter. He then consulted all the available editions of the Smṛti and found that excepting a few variants, there is no difference in the total number of verses. All these activities of the scholar have resulted in the outcome of the present book. For making the text of the *Laghu-Hārīta-Smṛti* more authentic and critical, he has consulted all the available seven editions of the text. Numerous manuscripts of the text are found in different manuscript-collections, but the editor has solely depended upon the printed editions for the present text, since the former are generally based upon them.

The editor has dealt with the important aspects like Hārīta, his date and his Smṛtis and specifically discussed the problem of its correlation and textual similarity with the *Narasiṁha Purāṇa*. Against Dr. Hazra, he has opined that the *Narasiṁha Purāṇa* is the borrower and the *Laghu-Hārīta-Smṛti* may be of an earlier date. Generally, Purāṇas seem to have assimilated and integrated into their corpus, the Smṛti-verses, which may be of earlier period.

The editor has given the text of the *Laghu-Hārīta-Smṛti* in *devanāgarī*, along with verse to verse English translation. He has also presented detailed notes, incorporating discussion on the variant readings and explanations of some words, from the point of view of Dharmaśāstra. In all these aspects he has tried to be as perfect and accurate as was possible to him with the help of available resources. The verse-index and the Bibliography given at the end of the book would be found useful.

The present edition of the *Laghu-Hārīta-Smṛti*, along with its Introduction, English translation and notes is no doubt an incomparable and a novel contribution to the hitherto published Dharmaśāstra literature, from the pen of a scholar of Purāṇa literature.

Holi,
Dt. 6.3.2004

M.L. Wadekar
Officiating Director,
Oriental Institute,
M.S. University of Baroda,
Vadodara.

Preface

Years back in 1980-81 when I was working on my dissertation "*Narasiṁha Purāṇa—A Study with Critical Introduction and Translation*, I got interested in a Smṛti-text called "*Laghu-Harita-Smṛti*. The redactor of the *Narasiṁha Purāṇa* has appropriated a large number of verses from the *Laghu-Harita-Smṛti*. So since then I had an earnest desire to bring out its critical edition provided opportunity favours me.

As far as I remember correctly, the P. G. Department of Sanskrit, Utkal University organised a state-level Seminar on *Smṛti* and *Karmakāṇḍa* on 8th May, 1998. There I presented a paper on the *Laghu-Harita-Smṛti* which was highly appreciated. Thereafter my young friend Dr. Subash Chandra Dash, Lecturer in Sanskrit, Utkal University used to encourage me for bringing out an authentic edition of this Smṛti-text. And it is because of his constant inspiration and insistence that the text in its present shape is going to be published after so many years.

This edition of the *Laghu-Harita-Smṛti* is based upon seven printed texts available at present. In the History of *Dharmaśāstra* Vol. I, part I, p. 134 Kane maintains that in Jīvānanda's collection *Laghu-Harita-Smṛti* contains about 250 verses, but in course of my investigation when I came across Jīvānanda's text where there is no numbering, I found that the total lines amount to 392 and they can be safely converted into 194 *ślokas* like other texts in my possession. So I am sure, *Laghu-Harita-Smṛti* has 7 Chapters and 194 verses in all. Though Pañcānana Tarkaratna has translated this text into Bengali in *Baṅgābda* 1300, M. N. Dutt into English in the year 1906 and Pt. Mihir Chand into Hindi [published in *Aṣṭādaśa Smṛti* (pp. 80-113), Nag Publishers, Delhi, 1990], I differ from them in the interpretation of some verses. Moreover, the numbering of verses by Mihir Chand is very defective particularly in Chapters III and IV. So a reliable edition of the *Laghu-Harita-Smṛti* was a desideratum of our time.

At the outset this humble attempt contains an Introduction focussing the importance of this Smṛti, its connection with *Hārīta-Gītā* and the *Narasiṁha Purāṇa*. A possible date for this text has also been added. It is then followed by the genuine text with English translation and exhaustive notes. In the end, index of *ślokas*, bibliography and the index of important words are appended for the benefit of Sanskrit scholars and general readers.

For the collection of different printed editions of Laghu-Harita-Smṛti, I am indebted to Prof. M. L. Wadekar and Dr. (Mrs) Sweta Prajapati, Oriental Institute, Baroda, Prof. B. K. Swain, Sri Jagannatha Sanskrit University, Puri and Dr. Niranjan Jena, C.A.S.S., Poona. During the period when this work was in rapid progress, it is Prof Wadekar who has actully helped me a lot. In fact I have no words to express my gratitude to him. In spite of his busy schedule he has spared sometime for me to go through it; and he has obliged me by writing a foreword to my work. Once again I extend my heart-felt thanks to him for his kind gestures shown to me. I am also thankful to Prof. G. K. Dash, Department of Sanskrit, Utkal University, Bhubaneswar for correctly interpreting three ambiguous verses of the *Laghu-Harita-Smṛti*. I put on record the ungrudging help and assistance of my former student Dr. Sulok Sundar Mohanty, now Reader-in-Sanskrit, N. C. College, Jajpur who, being a scholar of Smṛti literature has met my queries on certain dubious Smṛti-works and has offered very considered and cogent suggestions on some debatable Smṛti problems.

Lastly Mr. C. P. Gautam M/S Bharatiya Kala Prakashan, Delhi deserves all praise and admiration for taking up the publication of this work in right earnest and for bringing it out in time.

25.6.2004 **Siddheswar Jena**
Bhubaneshwar

Introduction

Śruti or Veda is a sum total of *Mantras* and Brāhmaṇas (*Mantra-Brāhmaṇayor Veda-nāmadheyam). Mantra* means a hymn addressed to some natural force or divinity. The collection of *Mantras* is called Saṁhitā. The Saṁhitās are four in number—*Ṛk*, *Sāma*, *Yajuḥ* and *Atharva*. They are compiled for the smooth performance of the Vedic sacrifices.

The Brāhmaṇas, unlike the *Mantras* are written in prose. They are the elaboration of the complicated rituals of the Vedas. They deal with rules and regulations for the practical performance of the rites and sacrifices. The *Mantras* and the Brāhmaṇas are called the *Karmakāṇḍa* as they deal with the sacrificial rituals. On the other hand, the Āraṇyakas and the Upaniṣads are called the *Jñāna-kāṇḍa* as they deal with the knowledge of the Self. Of the six systems of Indian philosophy, the *Mīmāṁsā* is connected with *Karmakāṇḍa*. It deals with earlier portion of the Vedas i.e. *Mantra* and Brāhmaṇa and is, therefore, called *Pūrva-Mīmāṁsā*. In contrast to Vedānta philosophy which deals with *Brahman*, it is related to *Dharma* and hence it is rightly called *Dharma-Mīmāṁsā*.

Smṛti is connected with *Dharma*. It reflects the socio-religious life of the Indian people through centuries. The historical evolution of the socio-religious life of the different people living in different parts of India and swearing allegiance to various forms of religion can be traced in the different Smṛti-texts composed at different periods of time. Smṛti literature in general records the activities of the Aryans so far as their every day life is concerned. For a proper understanding of the evolution of social and religious institutions through the ages, study of Smṛti literature is, in fact, indispensable. *History of Dharmaśāstra* Vols I-VIII by P. V. Kane is a monumental work in this regard.

In Smṛti-texts generally the manners and conduct are dealt with as they constitute the very essence of a cultured life. The major Smṛti-works are divided into three sections —*ācāra* (duties in general), *vyavahāra* (kingly duties and laws of punishment) and *prāyascitta* (expiation). The section on *ācāra* or duties in general is treated as the basis of social conduct.[1] It also includes the discussion of social and ethical codes. *Vyavahāra* stands for kingly duties and laws of punishment. It involves civil and criminal law and judicial procedure. The *prāyaścitta* or expiation is, however, a major issue with all the Smṛti-texts. They describe in detail the various types of sins and their consequences so that people may abstain from sins and take recourse to right path. The method of expiation for each type of sin or evil deed is elaborately treated in the Smṛtis.

The *Manu-Smṛti* and *Yājñavalkya* Smṛti are regarded as authoritative Smṛti-works on all the three aspects discussed above. Some *Smṛtikāras* like Baudhāyana, Vyāsa and Āśvalāyana attach importance only to *varṇāśrama-dharma* and expiation. In short, the aim and purpose of all the Smṛits is to provide people with a general social code of conduct which enables them to follow a pious and cultured way of life.

Coming to the law-maker Hārīta we may say that Hārīta was an ancient *Sūtrakāra* on *Dharma*. He was profusely quoted by Baudhāyana, Āpastamba, and Vasiṣṭha as an authority in their respective Dharmasūtras. As Kane mentions, it is Pt. Vamansastri Islampurkar who discovered a manuscript of *Hārīta-Dharmasūtra* at Nasik. It consists of 30 Chapters and from its contents and language it appears to be ancient. In this text the prose is mixed up with verses in Anustubh and Tristubh metres and the Kashmirian word *Kaphella* is cited here. From numerous quotations from Hārīta in the *Nibandhas* it seems that like other *Dharmasūtrakāras* he deals exhaustively with the same topics such as sources of *dharma*, two types of *brahmacārin*, *snātaka*, house-holder, forest-hermit, prohibitions about food, impurity on birth and death, *śrāddha*, general rules of conduct, the five *yajñas*, Vedic study, holidays and so on.

Hārīta not only refers to Vedas, Vedāṅgas and Dharmaśāstras, but also to many other branches of knowledge. As he quotes from each and every Veda, he does not belong to any specific Veda. And it is because of this that though Kumārila assigns Āpastamba and Baudhāyana to the Taittirīya school, he does not assign Hārīta to any particular school. He only takes the latter to be an ancient *Dharmasūtrakāra*.

Kane describes at length the quotations from Hārīta by various texts. The *Kṛtya-Kalpataru* of Lakṣmīdhara (1125-1145 A.D.) many a time quotes prose and verses from Hārīta. The *brahmacārikāṇda* guotes over 50 times and the *vyavahāra kāṇda* guotes over 70 times. It is Aparārka who makes both prose and verse quotations from Hārīta over 110 times. Thus it leads Kane to remark—'The Dharmasūtra of Hārīta appears to have been a very extensive one and was in mixed prose and verses[2].

Now, with regard to the Smṛti-text by Hārīta we notice that there are some four texts extant in his name—

i) *Laghu-Hārīta-Smṛti* containing 117 verses;

ii) *Vṛddha-Hārīta-Saṁhitā* containing 8 Chapters and about 2600 verses;

iii) Another *Laghu-Hārīta-Smṛti* dealing with *varṇ-āśramadharma* and *yoga*; and

iv) Hārīta-Saṁhitā.

Of these four the first one deals with purification from various kinds of pollution, *prāyaścittas*, rules about impurity on birth and death, *śrāddha* etc. It has been published in *Smṛtīnām Samuccayaḥ* (A.S.S.), Pune. The second one is an extensive Viṣṇuite work describing the *nitya* and *naimittika* rites of *varṇas* and *āśramas*, the method of worship of Viṣṇu, importance of twelve, sixteen, eighteen-syllabled *Mantras*, kingly duties and laws of punishment. Its sixth Chapter is mainly devoted to the account of sins and their expiation. This Saṁhitā has been published by Jīvānanda Vidyāsāgara in his collection *Dharmaśāstra-Saṁgraha* Vol. I (p. 194ff), Calutta. It is also found in *Dharmaśāstra-Saṁgraha* edited by Vachaspati Upadhyaya, a reprint of Mahadeva Shastri Amarpurkar's *Dharmaśāstra-Saṁgraha* (or *Aṣṭāviṁśati Smṛtayaḥ*), Jñāna Darpaṇa Press, Bombay. Under the title

Vṛddha-Hārīta-Smṛti it is again published in *Smṛti-Sandarbha*, Part-II (p. 994 ff) by Manasukharaya Mor, Calcutta. The third and the fourth one are textually the same even though they go by different names. Each of them contains 7 Chapters and 194 *ślokas*. Both deal with the same theme. And we are very much concerned about this text since it is taken up here for its critical reconstruction. The present edition is based upon the following seven printed texts available with us.

i) *Laghu-Hārīta-Smṛti*—It forms a text in the collection *Dharmaśāstra-Saṁgraha* Vol. I by Jīvānanda Vidyāsāgara. Printed in *devanāgarī* character it is published in Calcutta in the year 1876. The verses of this text are not enumerated.

ii) *Hārīta-Saṁhitā*—It is noticed in the collection known as *Unaviṁśati-Saṁhitā* edited by Pañcānana Tarkaratna and published by Baṇgavāsi press, Calcutta in *Baṇgābda* 1300. Printed in Bengali character it is translated into simple Bengali prose. The *ślokas* in this text are serially enumerated.

iii) *Hārīta-Saṁhitā*—It contains the text in *devanāgarī* script with a literal prose translation in English. It is edited and published by M. N. Dutt in Calcutta in 1906. Here there is the enumeration of Sanskrit verses.

iv) *Laghu-Hārīta-Smṛti*—Printed in *devanāgarī* character it appears in the second part of *Smṛti-Sandarbha* (pp. 974-994). Published by Manasukharaya Mor in Calcutta in the year 1957, the verses of this text are numbered.

v) *Laghu-Hārīta-Smṛti*—It is included in the collection "*Aṣṭādaśa-Smṛti*" edited by Pt. Mihir Chand. Nag Publishers, Delhi have published this volume in 1990. Though printed in *devanāgarī* script with Hindi translation, the numbering of the *ślokas* in the text seems to be defective particularly in Chapters III and IV.

vi) *Laghu-Hārīta-Smṛti*—It is found in the collection "*Dharmaśāstra-Saṁgraha*" or "*Aṣṭāviṁśati Smṛtyaḥ*" edited by Pt. Mahadeva Shastri Amarpurkar. Printed at Jñāna Darpaṇa Press, Bombay in Śaka era1809 it provides only the bare text, the verses of which are not enumerated.

vii) *Laghu-Hārīta-Smṛti*—It is a part of the collection "*Dharmaśāstra-Saṁgraha*" Vol. I edited by Vachaspati Upadhyaya. Published by Navarang, Delhi in 1982 it is simply a reprint of Mahadeva Shastri Amarpurkar's *Dharmaśāstra-Saṁgraha* or *Aṣṭāviṁśati Smṛtayaḥ*. Printed in *devanāgarī* character when Pt. Shastri gives only the bare text, the text of Upadhyaya goes with a subject index and an introduction in the beginning. The verses of this text are also not numbered.

As has been pointed out above, both the texts—*Laghu-Hārīta-Smṛti* and *Hārīta-Saṁhitā* are identical. The word "Saṁhitā" has different meanings. According to the Sanskrit-English Dictionary of V. S. Apte "any systematically arranged collection of texts or verses is known as Saṁhitā". It further adds that a compendium or compilation of laws, codes or digest is also known as Saṁhitā[3]. The *Śabdakalpadruma* also defines this word in the following manner—सम्यक् हितं प्रतिपाद्यं यस्याः[4] i.e. Saṁ*hitā* is that text which contains something quite wholesome. Thus the word Saṁhitā is found to be appropriately used in favour of law-texts that give wholesome advice for the well-being of the man. The *Manu-Saṁhitā*, the *Atri-Saṁhitā*, the *Vyāsa-Saṁhitā*, the *Dakṣa-Saṁhitā*, the *Gautama-Saṁhitā*, the *Śātātapa-Saṁhitā*, the *Vaśiṣṭha-Saṁhitā*, the *Likhita-Saṁhitā*, and the *Bṛhat-Parāśara-Saṁhitā* are the glaring instances of it.

It is needless to say that this word "Saṁhitā" was very popular in the Vedic age. Out of the four parts of a Veda, the first part namely the collection of hymns is known as Saṁhitā. So it seems probable that ancient law-makers have designated their literary output as Saṁhitā in order to add to their value.

Following the defination of *Śabda-kalpadruma* the term "Saṁhitā" is also applicable to all the Dharmaśāstras. Thus it is quite clear that our ancient authors of law have freely used the words "Smṛti", "*Saṁhitā*" and "Dharma-śāstra" to denote their law-works and sometimes even they have interchangeably made use of these three terms for one and the same work. For example, though the text is the same, *Laghu-Hārīta-Smṛti* is given the name *Hārīta-Saṁhitā* and the colophon of each of seven Chapters of this book ends with—"इति हारीते धर्मशास्त्रे....अध्यायः"। On the other hand the text of Vṛddha-Hārīta is popularly known as *Vṛddha-Hārīta* Saṁhitā[5] and interestingly the colophon at the end of most of the Chapters of this text ends with—"इति वृद्धहारीत स्मृतौ विशिष्टधर्मशास्त्रे....नाम...अध्यायः"। Besides, at some places it is also published under the caption *Vṛddha-Hārīta-Smṛti* just as we notice in the collection "*Smṛti-Sandarbha*" Part II p. 994 ff. Anyway out of the seven printed texts used here for an authentic edition, since the five texts are in favour of the caption "*Laghu-Hārīta-Smṛti*", so we prefer it to *Hārīta-Saṁhitā* and we would like to retain it instead of the latter. Now let us have a look at the contents of *Laghu-Hārīta-Smṛti*.

In the prefatory verses of *Laghu-Hārīta-Smṛti* we notice that sages request Hārīta to describe the duties of various *varṇas* and *āśramas* and also the *yoga-śāstra* and everything that would arouse faith in Viṣṇu. Accordingly Hārīta gives his well-thought out opinion on all the topics.

The first Chapter deals with the creation of the universe and the duties of *brāhmaṇas*, the second Chapter describes the duties of three other *varṇas* namely *kṣatriyas*, *vaiśyas* and *śūdras*. The four *āśramas* of life e.g. *brahmacarya*, *gārhasthya*, *vānaprastha* and *sannyāsa* are dealt with in the third, fourth, fifth and sixth Chapters respectively. And essence of *yoga* (*yogasāra*) is the subject matter of the last Chapter.

This last Chapter is very important and it lays great stress on the practice of *yoga*. It holds that all the sins are absolved by the power of *yoga*. Hence one should practise meditation in course of performing all religious rites. Seated in a solitary place with concentrated mind one should till death, meditate on the Self who is both immanent and transcendent. And meditation is required to continue till the attainment of bliss of self-realisation. Then through nice examples the *Smṛtikāra* describes that just as a chariot is useless without horses and the horses are of no use without a charioteer, both *tapas* and knowledge constitute an infallible medicine for the suffering of the world[6]. A bird can fly about in the sky with the help of its two wings only. So like a man gets the vision of eternal *Brahman* through both knowledge and action[7]. A *brāhmaṇa* endowed with knowledge and *tapas*, devoted to the practice of *yoga*, is immediately freed from the fetters of *saṁsāra*[8].

Besides, the style of this Smṛti is lucid and the expressions are very clear and distinct. In Chapter I. 25 the author of the text nicely shows the intimate relation of both *Śruti* and Smṛti. He asserts that "Śruti and Smṛti" are the two eyes of the *brāhmaṇas* created by god. Without the knowledge of one a person becomes one-eyed (*kāṇaḥ*) whereas bereft of both he turns to be blind (*andhaḥ*)[9].

Owing to sweet and simple language, clarity of thought and expressions once upon a time the Smṛti-texts of Hārīta were very popular among the masses. *Laghu-Hārīta-Smṛti* being a handy book on *ācāra* or general duties of *varṇas* and *āśramas* was not only widely read and followed, but it exerted a great influence on the general public. People regulated their daily life in conformity with its precepts. And for this reason Hārīta was profusely quoted by the *Nibandhakāras*. As a *Smṛtikāra* Hārīta was so renowned and influential that in course of time his dialogue with the sages or say his precepts found a place in the *Mahābhārata* in the form of *Hārīta-Gītā*. Because of his firm hold on people, the redactor of the great epic, like other renowned sages such as Utathya, Maṅki, Parāśara and Vāmadeva etc. could not ignore him.

Laghu-Hārīta-Smṛti and Hārīta-Gītā

Apart from the famous *Bhagavad-Gītā* many other Gītās are noticed in the *Mahābhārata*. They are *Utathya-Gītā*, *Vāmadeva-Gītā*, *Samyāka-Gītā*, *Maṅki-Gītā*, *Parāśara-Gītā*, *Vicakhnu-Gītā* etc. And *Hārīta-Gītā* is represented by Chapter-269, Śānti-parvan of the *Mahābhārata*. Like *Laghu-Hārīta-Smṛti* this Gītā lays emphasis on proper code of conduct and righteous way of life that lead to emancipation. It says that one desirous of liberation should restrain his senses. Retiring from home, disregarding all objects of enjoyment and considering loss and gain on equal footing, he should adopt a life of renunciation. Neither with eye nor with word nor in thought he should disparage anybody. He should not speak ill of any person either directly or indirectly. He should also abstain from injuring any creature. Even when enraged by others, he should not utter angry words. Calumniated by another, he should not calumniate in return. He should not go about visiting many houses in his round of mendicancy. The man of restrained senses should seek alms in a house-holder's abode when the smoke has ceased to rise any more; when the fire in the hearth is extinguished; and when all the inmates have finished their meals. He should collect food as much as is barely necessary for keeping his body and soul together. A deserted house, the foot of a tree, a forest or a cave should be his place of habitation. Away from company, associated with *yoga* he should remain engaged in the recitation of sacred *mantras*. Controlling his mind, wrath, hunger and lust he should never allow the censures of others to afflict his heart. Keeping himself aloof from all attachments he should remain indifferent to praise or blame. In the words of Hātīta such a life of renunciation actually leads to the attainment of liberation.

Laghu-Hārīta-Smṛti* and the *Narasiṁha Purāṇa

The *Laghu-Hārīta-Smṛti* refers to Lord Narasiṁha at four places[10] in the text. It holds that performance of particular duties of *varṇas* and *āśramas* always propitiates Narasiṁha[11]. The Lord is not so much pleased with any other act as he is pleased with strict adherence to one's own duties in keeping with one's *varṇa* and *āśrama*[12]. He who punctiliously follows the duties of his *varṇa* and *āśrama*, undoubtedly goes to the abode of Narasiṁha[13] Besides, a house-holder is also said to be blessed with the highest wisdom by the grace of the Lord (ज्ञानोत्क षश्च तस्य स्यान्नारसिंहप्रसादत: Ch. IV. 76). And it won't be out of place if we add here that because of the leaning of *Laghu-Hārīta-Smṛti* towards Viṣṇu-Narasiṁha, it has been verbatim included in the *Narasiṁha Purāṇa* to suit its own theme.

The *Narasiṁha Purāṇa* is an Upa-purāṇa of about the middle of 13th century A.D.[14] meant for the glorification of Narasiṁha, the fourth incarnation of Viṣṇu. The redactor of *Narasiṁha Purāṇa* seems to have cleverly appropriated the entire *Laghu-Hārīta-Smṛti*, this small and handy text word for word in order to enhance the value of his Purāṇa. It is Prof. Hazra who propounds a wrong view that Ch. 57.8-Ch. 61 of the *Narasiṁha Purāṇa* are taken off and given the form of an independent work under the title *Hārīta-Saṁhitā* or *Laghu-Hārīta-Smṛti* which derives its name from the orignal speaker Hārīta[15], but it is untenable since at the time of composition of the

Narasiṁha Purāṇa Laghu-Hārīta-Smṛti was an earlier extant text and it was popular too. Besides, the *Purāṇa-kāras* were in the habit of borrowing from the Smṛti-texts at that time. So there is no doubt about the fact that the redactor of the *Narasiṁha Purāṇa* has inserted the most popular *Laghu-Hārīta-Smṛti* owing to its leaning towards Viṣṇu-Narasiṁha. Let us take a few concrete examples how the redactor of Narasiṁha has modified some verses of *Laghu-Hārīta-Smṛti* without affecting the meaning in order to serve his own purpose.

Laghu-Hārīta-Smṛti

वर्णानामाश्रमाणाञ्च धर्मान्नो ब्रूहि सत्तम।
येन सन्तुष्यते देवो नारसिंहः सनातनः।।१.२

इत्येष धर्मः कथितो मयायं
पृष्टो भवद्भिस्त्वखिलाघहारी।
वदामि राज्ञामपि चैव धर्मान्
पृथक् पृथग्बोधत विप्रवर्य्याः।। १.३२

वर्णेषु धर्मा विविधा मयोक्ता
यथा तथा ब्रह्ममुखेरिताः पुरा।
शृणुध्वमत्राश्रमधर्ममाद्यं
मयोच्यमानं क्रमशो मुनीन्द्राः।। २.१५

यो ब्रह्मचारी विधिना समाहितश्चरेत्
पृथिव्यां गुरुसेवने रतः।
संप्राप्य विद्यामतिदुर्लभां शिवां
फलञ्च तस्याः सुलभं तु विन्दति।। ३.१७

अभावे दन्तकाष्ठानां प्रतिषिद्धदिनेषु च।
अपां द्वादशगण्डूषैर्मुखशुद्धिं समाचरेत्।। ४.११

अकृते वैश्वदेवेऽपि भिक्षौ च गृहमागते।
उद्धृत्य वैश्वदेवार्थं भिक्षां दत्त्वा विसर्जयेत्।।
वैश्वदेवाकृतान् दोषाञ्छक्तो भिक्षुर्व्यपोहितुम्। ४.६१,-६२क

एवं हि विप्राः! कथितो मया वः
समासतः श्राश्वतधर्मराश्विः।
गृही गृहस्थस्य सतो हि धर्मं
कुर्वन् प्रयत्नाद्धरिमेति युक्तम्।। ४.७७

गृहस्थः पुत्रपौत्रादीन् दृष्टवा पलितमात्मनः।
भार्य्यां पुत्रेषु निःक्षिप्य सह वा प्रविशद्वनम्।। ५.२

तपो हि यः सेवति वन्यवासः
समाधियुक्तः प्रयतान्तरात्मा।
विमुक्तपापो विमलः प्रशान्तः
स याति दिव्यं पुरुषं पुराणम्।। ५.१०

एवं वनाश्रमे तिष्ठन् पातयंश्चैव किल्विषम्।
चतुर्थमाश्रमं गच्छेत् संन्यासविधिना द्विजः।। ६.२

सूर्यादिभूतदेवेभ्यो दत्त्वा संप्रोक्ष्य वारिणा।
भुञ्जीत पात्रपुटके पात्रे वा वाग्यतो यतिः।
वटकाश्वत्थपर्णेषु कुम्भीतैन्दुकपात्रके।।
कोविदारकदम्बेषु न भुञ्जीयात् कदाचन।
मलाक्ताः सर्व उच्यन्ते यतयः कांस्यभोजिनः।। ६.१५ख-१७

धर्मशास्त्रमिदं सर्वं हारीतमुखनिःसृतम्।
अधीत्य कुरुते धर्मं स यति परमां गतिम्।।

ब्राह्मणस्य तु यत् कर्म कथितं बाहुजस्य च।
ऊरुजस्यापि यत् कर्म्म कथितं पादजस्य च
अन्यथा वर्तमानस्तु सद्यः पतति जातितः।। ७.१५-१६

उत्पन्नवैराग्यबलेन योगी
ध्यायेत्परं ब्रह्म सदा क्रियावान्।
सत्यं सुखं रूपमनन्तमाद्यं
विहाय देहं पदमेति विष्णोः।। ७.२१

Narasiṁha Purāṇa

वर्णानामाश्रमाणाञ्च धर्मं मे वक्तुमर्हसि।
यैः कृतैस्तुष्यते देवो नरसिंहः सनातनः।। ५७.९

इत्येष धर्मः कथितो मया वै
विप्रस्य विप्रा अखिलाघहारी।
वदामि राजादिजनस्य धर्मं
पृथक् पृथग्बोधत विप्रवर्याः।। ५७.३०

वर्णेषु धर्मा विविधा मयोक्ता
यथाक्रमं ब्राह्मणवर्यसाधिताः।
शृणुध्वमत्राश्रमधर्ममाद्यं,
मयोच्यमानं क्रमशो मुनीन्द्राः।। ५८.१६

यो ब्रह्मचारी विधिमेतमास्थित-
श्चरेत्पृथिव्यां गुरुसेवने रतः।
संप्राप्य विद्यामपि दुर्लभां तां
फलं हि तस्याः सकलं हि विन्दति।। ५८.३८

अलाभे दन्तकाष्ठस्य प्रतिषिद्धे च तद्दिने।
अपां द्वादशगण्डूषैर्मुखशुद्धिर्विधीयते।। ५८.५१ख-५२क

अकृते वैश्वदेवे तु भिक्षौ भिक्षार्थमागते।
उद्धृत्य वैश्वदेवान्न भिक्षां दत्त्वा विसर्जयेत्।
वैश्वदेवाकृतं दोषं शक्तो भिक्षु व्यपोहितुम्।। ५८.१००क, १०१

एवं हि विप्राः कथितो मया वः
समासतः शाश्वतधर्मराशिः।
सम्यग्गृहस्थस्य सतो हि धर्मं
कुर्वन् प्रयत्नाद्धरिमेति मुक्तः।। ५८.११५

गृहस्थः पुत्रपौत्रादीन्दृष्ट्वा पलितमात्मनः।
स्वभार्यां तनये स्थाप्य स्वशिष्यैः प्रविशद्वनम्। ५९.२

तपो हि यः सेवति काननस्थो
वसेन्महत्सत्त्वसमाधियुक्तः।
विमुक्तपापो हि मनः प्रशान्तः
प्रयाति विष्णोः सदनं द्विजेन्द्रः।। ५९.१०

एवं वनाश्रमे तिष्ठंस्तपसा दग्धकिल्बिषः
चतुर्थमाश्रमं गच्छेत्संन्यस्य विधिना द्विजः।। ६०.२

सूर्यादि दैवतेभ्यो हि दत्त्वान्नं प्रोक्ष्य वारिणा।
भुञ्जीत पर्णपुटके पात्रे वा वाग्यतो यतिः।।
वटकाश्वत्थपत्रेषु कुम्भीतिन्दुकपत्रयोः।
कोविदारकरञ्जेषु न भुञ्जीत कदाचन।।
पलाशाः सर्व उच्यन्ते यतयः कांस्यभोजिनः।।

६०.१४-१५, १७क

धर्मशास्त्रमिदं यस्तु हारीतमुखनिस्सृतम्।
श्रुत्वा च कुरुते धर्मं स यति परमां गतिम्।।
मुखजस्य तु यत्कर्म कर्म यद्बाहुजस्य तु।
ऊरुजस्य तु यत्कर्म पादजस्य तथा नृप।।
अन्यथा वर्तमानो हि सद्यः पतति यात्यधः।

६१.१६-१७, १८ख

उत्पन्नवैराग्यबलेन योगाद्
ध्यायेत्परं ब्रह्म सदा क्रियावान्।
सत्यात्मकं चित्सुखरूपमाद्यं
विहाय देहं पदमेति विष्णोः।। ६१.२२

In this way many[16] more examples can be cited. It is evident that the *Narasiṁha Purāṇa* has not been able to resist the impact of *Hārīta-Smṛti* on the then society. Therefore we are rather sure, the *Narasiṁha Purāṇa* has borrowed from the *Laghu-Hārīta-Smṛti.*

Another problem that we confront here is about the terms—"Laghu", "Vṛddha", or "Bṛhat" pre-fixed to the Smṛti-texts. Our text goes by the name *Laghu-Hārīta-Smṛti*. *Vṛddha-Hārīta-Saṁhitā* or *Vṛddha-Hārīta-Smṛti* is also available.While discussing the *Hārīta-Dharmasūtra* in the *History of Dharmaśāstra* Vol. I Part I, Kane refers to the remarks of some early commentators and digest-writers when he says that "Manu and Vṛddha-Manu, Yājñavalkya and Vṛddha-Yājñavalkya and the like were not entirely different individuals but they were the same authors at different stages of their lives[17]. Again he holds that Vṛddha-Hārīta in prose is cited by *Mitākṣarā* on Yājñavalkya III. 259, 261 and the Vṛddha-Hārīta in verse is a comparatively late work, for it distinctly quotes from the Smṛtis of Manu, Yājñavalkya, Nārada and Kātyāyana as authorities on *rāja-dharma*[18]. Since various versions of Smṛti-texts of Hārīta are available (vide Supra, pp. 4-6), it seems that several compilations have been made at different times and ascribed to Hārīta, because they are based more or less on the *Hārīta-Dharmasūtra*[19] that was originally written in mixed prose and verse (vide Supra, p. 4). And in the end Kane concludes that long before sixth century A.D. the *Hārīta-Dharmasūtra* contained verses.[20]

Now, it is noteworthy to refer to the views of another scholar Derrett who speaks on Laghu-Smṛti and Vṛddha-Smṛti works that "from ninth century on, irrespective of the development of Purāṇic material, a new wave of Smṛti writing occurred. The names given to the works, often pre-fixed (as were some older works) with Vṛddha,-Laghu- and so on are chosen from the list of known authors of genuine Smṛtis" (*Dharmaśāstra and Juridical Literature*, p. 40). Thus we not only find *Laghu-Hārīta-Smṛti and Vṛddha-Hārīta-Smṛti*, but also a number of texts come to our notice such as *Laghu-Atri-Saṁhitā, Vṛddha-Ātreya-Saṁhita, Bṛhat-Parāśara-Saṁhitā, Vṛddha-Gautama-Saṁhitā, Laghu-Vyāsa-Saṁhitā, Laghv-Āśvalāyana-Smṛti, Laghu-Yama-Smṛti and Laghu-Budha-Smṛti* etc. So we would like to conclude that most possibly our text under discussion may be a product between 600-900 A.D.

NOTES

1. आचारो परमो धर्मः सर्वेषामिति निश्चयः।
   हीनाचारपरीतात्मा प्रेत्य चेह च नश्यति।।
   Śrīvāsiṣṭha-Dharmaśāstram-6.1

2. Kane, P.V.—History of Dharmaśāstra-Vol.I., Part-I, p. 133.
3. Apte, V.S.—The Practical Sanskrit-English Dictionary-Vol. III, p. 1599.
4. Deva, Raja Radhakanta—Śabda-ka padruma, Vol. V, p. 208.
5. Vide Vidyāsāgara, Jīvānanda-*Dharmaśāstra-Saṁgraha*, Vol. I pp. 194-409.
   Amarpurkar Mahadeva Shastri-*Dharmaśāstra-Saṁgraha* pp. 161-320.
   Upadhyaya, Vachaspati-*Dharmaśāstra-Saṁgraha*, Vol. I pp. 161-320.
6. यथा रथोऽश्वहीनस्तु यथाश्वो रथिहीनकः।
   एवं तपश्च विद्या च संयुतं भैषजं भवेत्।।
   Laghu-Hārita-Smṛti, Ch. VII. 9.
7. उभाभ्यामपि पक्षाभ्यां यथा खे पक्षिणां गतिः।
   तथैव ज्ञानकर्मभ्यां प्राप्यते ब्रह्म शाश्वतम्।। Ibid., Ch. VII. 10b-11 a.
8. Ibid., Ch. VII. 11b-12a.
9. श्रुतिस्मृती च विप्राणां चक्षुषी देवनिर्मिते।
   काणः तत्र एकया हीनो द्वाभ्यां अन्धः प्रकीर्तितः।। *Laghu-Hārita-Smṛti-*, Ch. I.25.
10. *Laghu-Hārita-Smṛti*—Ch. I.2, Ch. II.9, Ch. IV.76, Ch. VII. 19-20.
11. वर्णानामाश्रमाणाञ्च धर्मान्......................।
    येन सन्तुष्यते देवो नारसिंहः सनातनः।।
    Laghu-Hārīta-Smṛti, Ch. I.2.
12. स्वधर्मेण यथा नृणां नारसिंहः प्रसीदति।
    न तुष्यति तथान्येन कर्मणा मधुसूदनः।। Ibid., Ch. VII.19.
13. अतः कुर्वन्निजं कर्म्म यथाकालमतन्द्रितः।।
    सहस्रानीकदेवेशं नारसिंहञ्च सालयम्।।Ibid., Ch. VII.20.
14. For Details Vide Jena, S.—*The Narasiṁha Purāṇa*—A Study, Ch. II, p.16.

15. Vide Hazra, R.C.—*Studies in the Upa-purāṇas,* Vol. I, 260.
16. Vide Jena, S—*Textual Correlation of Narasiṁha Purāṇa with other Purāṇas and Sanskrit-texts* pp. 81-96.
17. Kane, P.V.—*History of Dharmaśāstra,* Vol. I, Part. I, p. 135.
18. Ibid, pp. 134-135.
19. Ibid, p. 135.
20. Kane, P.V.—*History of Dharmaśāstra,* Vol. I, Part-I, p. 136.

लघुहारीतस्मृतिः

CHAPTER - I

Essential characteristics of the devotees of Viṣṇu etc.

ये वर्णाश्रमधर्मस्थास्ते भक्ताः केशवं प्रति।
इति पूर्वं त्वया प्रोक्तं भुर्भूवःस्वर्द्विजोत्तमाः॥१॥

You have told me before that those foremost of the twice-born[1] ones who reside on the earth, the atmospheric and celestial regions and perform their duties in keeping with their *varṇas* and *āśramas*, happen to be the real devotees of Keśava (Viṣṇu).(1)

वर्णानामाश्रमाणाञ्च धर्मान्नो ब्रूहि सत्तम।
येन सन्तुष्यते देवो नारसिंहः सनातनः॥२॥

O most righteous one ! now tell us for different *varṇas* and *āśramas*, what are the peculiar duties the performance of which leads to the propitiation of the eternal lord Narasiṁha.(2)

मार्कण्डेय उवाच
अत्राहं कथयिष्यामि पुरावृत्तमनुत्तमम्।
ऋषिभिः सह संवादं हारीतस्य महात्मनः॥३॥

Mārkaṇḍeya replied :

High—souled Hārīta had discussed this question with the sages. Now I would narrate to you that old and unique discourse of the past.(3)

हारीतं सर्वधर्मज्ञमासीनमिव पावकम्।
प्रणिपत्याब्रुवन् सर्वे मुनयो धर्मकाङ्क्षिणः॥४॥

Once it so happened that all the sages with the desire of getting some knowledge of *dharma* approached the revered sage Hārīta who was effulgent like the fire and who was the knower of the essence of *dharma*; they fell at his feet and asked :—(4)

भगवन्! सर्वधर्मज्ञ! सर्वधर्मप्रवर्त्तक!।
वर्णानामाश्रमाणाञ्च धर्मान्नो ब्रूहि भार्गव॥५॥

O lord, O scion of Bhṛgu race! you are the best knower of righteousness; you are the most eminent propounder of it. Please advise us as to what are the duties prescribed for people of different *varṇas* and *āśramas*.(5)

समासाद्योगशास्त्रञ्च विष्णुभक्तिकरं परम्।
एतच्चान्यच्च भगवन्! ब्रूहि नः परमो गुरुः॥६॥

O lord, O great preceptor! tell us, in brief, the *Yogaśāstra* and other things that lead to create firm faith in Viṣṇu.(6)

हारीतस्तानुवाचाथ तैरेवं चोदितो मुनिः।
शृण्वन्तु मुनयः! सर्वे! धर्मान् वक्ष्यामि शाश्वतान्॥७॥

Having been thus requested, then the sage Hārīta

said to them—'O sages! I am describing the eternal duties. You all listen to me'.(7)

वर्णानामाश्रमाणाञ्च योगशास्त्रञ्च सत्तमाः!।

सन्धार्य्य मुच्यते मर्त्यो जन्मसंसारबन्धनात्॥८॥

By adhering to the precepts of *Yogaśāstra* and the duties of *varṇas* and *āśramas* as well, O most righteous ones! a mortal is freed from the fetters of birth and mundane existence.(8)

पुरा देवो जगत्स्रष्टा परमात्मा जलोपरि।

सुष्वाप भोगिपर्यङ्के शयने तु श्रिया सह॥९॥

In the days of yore the Supreme Soul (Viṣṇu), the creator of the universe along with His spouse Śrī (Lakṣmī) had His sleep on the couch of serpent Ananta lying on that huge unfathomable ocean.(9)

तस्य सुप्तस्य नाभौ तु महत् पद्ममभूत् किल।

पद्ममध्येऽभवद् ब्रह्मा वेदवेदाङ्गभूषणः॥१०॥

When He was asleep, a great lotus sprang forth from His navel and seated on the lotus there appeared Brahmā proficient in the knowledge of the Vedas and Vedāṅgas.(10)

स चोक्तो देवदेवेन जगत्सृज पुनः पुनः।

सोऽपि सृष्ट्वा जगत् सर्वं सदेवासुरमानुषम्॥११॥

Viṣṇu, the Lord of gods time and again advised Brahmā—'Go on creating the universe'. And accordingly He created the entire universe consisting of gods, demons and human beings.(11)

यज्ञसिद्ध्यर्थमनघान् ब्राह्मणान्मुखतोऽसृजत्।
असृजत् क्षत्रियान् बाह्वोर्वैश्यानप्युरुदेशतः॥१२॥
शूद्रांश्च पादयोः सृष्ट्वा तेषां चैवानुपूर्वशः।
यथा प्रोवाच भगवान् ब्रह्मयोनिं पितामहः॥१३॥
तद्वचः संप्रवक्ष्यामि शृणुत द्विजसत्तमाः!।
धन्यं यशस्यमायुष्यं स्वर्ग्यं मोक्षफलप्रदम्॥१४॥

For successful performance of sacrifices Brahmā, first of all, created the pious *brāhmaṇas* from his mouth. From his arms, thighs and feet respectively, He created the *kṣatriyas* the *vaiśyas* and the *śudras*. (Having created these four *varṇas*) Lord Brahmā, the progenitor of the world told some words to Viṣṇu, his ultimate source and origin (*Brahma-yoni*). Now I would narrate to you those words of Brahmā. O righteous *brāhmaṇas*! listen to those words that *bestow* wealth, fame and longevity. Heaven and liberation too are within one's easy reach.(12-14)

ब्राह्मण्यां ब्राह्मणेनैव मुत्पन्नो ब्राह्मणः स्मृतः।
तस्य धर्मं प्रवक्ष्यामि तद्योग्य देशमेव च॥१५॥

A child born from a *brāhmaṇa* mother through a *brāhmaṇa* father is really a *brāhmaṇa*; now I am speaking of his conduct of life and the place worthy of his habitation.(15)

कृष्णसारो मृगो यत्र स्वभावेन प्रवर्त्तते।
तस्मिन् देशे वसेद्धर्मः सिद्ध्यति द्विजसत्तमाः॥१६॥

O revered twice-born ones! it behoves a *brāhmaṇa* to live in the place where the spotted antelopes move freely and fearlessly, for religious practices attain success there.(16)

षट् कर्माणि निजान्याहुर्ब्राह्मणस्य महात्मनः।
तैरेव सततं यस्तु वर्त्तयेत् सुखमेधते॥१७॥
अध्यापनं चाध्ययनं याजनं यजनं तथा।
दानं प्रतिग्रहश्चेति षट्कर्माणीति चोच्यते॥१८॥

A *brāhmaṇa* who is constantly engaged in performing the six duties prescribed for him, gets happiness and prosperity. Study (of the Vedas), advancement of learning by teaching the Vedic lore to others, performance of sacrifices and officiating as priest in the sacrifices of members of his own caste or others, making gifts and acceptance of gifts—these are the six duties prescribed for a high-souled *brāhmaṇa*.(17-18)

अध्यापनञ्च त्रिविधं धर्मार्थमृक्थकारणात्।
शुश्रूषाकरणञ्चेति त्रिविधं परिकीर्त्तितम्॥१९॥

Teaching of the Vedas can be taken up for three reasons—for acquiring religious merit, for wealth (*ṛktha*) and for getting the service of his disciples.(19)

एषामन्यतमाभावे वृषाचारो भवेद् द्विजः।
तत्र विद्या न दातव्या पुरुषेण हितैषिणा॥२०॥

In the absence of at least one of these purposes and with a different purpose other than the above three, a *brāhmaṇa* becomes as ignominious as a *śūdra* (vṛṣācāra).

In such a state teaching should not be imparted by a person seeking his own welfare and well-being.(20)

योग्यानध्यापयेच्छिष्यानयोग्यानपि वर्जयेत्।

विदितात् प्रतिगृह्णीयाद् गृहे धर्मप्रसिद्धये॥२१॥

A *brāhmaṇa* should impart teaching only to the selected worthy disciples and discard the unworthy fellows. For leading a meaningful house-holder's life he should accept gifts only from a known person freed from sins.(21)

वेदञ्चैवाभ्यसेन्नित्यं शूचौ देशे समाहितः।

धर्मशास्त्रं तथा पाठ्यं ब्राह्मणैः शुद्धमानसैः॥२२॥

Seated in a sanctified place in a composed state of mind he should daily study the Vedas. *Dharmaśāstras* should be similarly studied by the pure-minded *brāhmaṇas*.(22)

वेदवत्पठितव्यं च श्रोतव्यञ्च दिवा निशि।

स्मृतिहीनाय विप्राय श्रुतिहीने तथैव च।

दानं भोजनमन्यच्च दत्तं कुलविनाशनम्॥२३॥

Like the Vedas *Dharmaśāstras* should be read aloud and listened to day and night. Making gifts and offering food and other things to a *brāhmaṇa* who is devoid of knowledge of both '*Śruti*' and '*Smṛti*' leads to the destruction of one's family.(23)

तस्मात् सर्वप्रयत्नेन धर्मशास्त्रं पठेद् द्विजः।

श्रुतिस्मृतो च विप्राणां चक्षुषी देवनिर्मिते।
काणस्तत्रैकया हीनो द्वाभ्यामन्धः प्रकीर्त्तितः॥२४॥

Hence a *brāhmaṇa* should, with all care, read out the *Dharmaśāstra*. The *Śruti* and *Smṛti* are said to be the two eyes of the *brāhmaṇas* created by God. A person deprived of the knowledge of one, is called one-eyed (*kāṇaḥ*) whereas he, devoid of both, is regarded as blind (*andhaḥ*).(24)

गुरुश्शुश्रूषणञ्चैव यथान्यायमतन्द्रितः।
सायं प्रातरुपासीत विवाहाग्निं द्विजोत्तमः॥२५॥

Without giving himself to stupor he should attend upon his preceptors in accordance with the principles of propriety and decorum. Besides, daily in the morning and in the evening a devout *brāhmaṇa* should adore the sacred *vivāha*-fire.(25)

सुस्नातस्तु प्रकुर्वीत वैश्वदेवं दिने दिने।
अतिथीनागताञ्छक्त्या पूजयेदविचारतः॥२६॥

Daily after proper bath one should offer Vaiśvadeva sacrifice[4] and treat, according to one's means, the incoming guests without any discrimination.(26)

अन्यानभ्यागतान् विप्राः! पूजयेच्छक्तितो गृही।
स्वदारनिरतो नित्यं परदारविवर्जितः॥२७॥
कृतहोमस्तु भुञ्जीत सायं प्रातरुदारधीः।
सत्यवादी जितक्रोधो नाधर्मे वर्त्तयेन्मतिम्॥२८॥

O *brāhmaṇas*! a house-holder should, with all honour, treat the other guests according to his means. Constantly devoted to one's own wife without the least attachment for others wives, truthful and free from anger, a *brāhmaṇa* should withdraw his mind from unrighteousness. After offering oblations to the fire daily in the morning and in the evening, the liberal-minded *brāhmaṇa* should take his meal.(27-28)

स्वकर्मणि च संप्राप्ते प्रमादान्न निवर्त्तते।

सत्यां हितां वदेद्वाचं परलोकहितैषिणीम्॥२९॥

Conscientiously doing one's duties one should not desist from it through carelessness; one should speak true yet beneficial words which alone are conducive to a happy life in the other world.(29)

एष धर्मः समुद्दिष्टो ब्राह्मणस्य समासतः।

धर्ममेव हि यः कुर्यात् स याति ब्रह्मणः पदम्॥३०॥

This is, in brief, the code of conduct for a *brāhmaṇa*; and the *brāhmaṇa* who adheres to this code of conduct, goes to the abode of Brahmā.(30)

इत्येष धर्मः कथितो मयायं पृष्टो भवद्भिस्त्वखिलाघहारी।

वदामि राज्ञामपि चैव धर्मान् पृथक् पृथग्बोधत विप्र-

वर्य्याः॥३१॥

As you have put questions I have accordingly expounded to you the code of conduct that is destructive of all sins. O virtuous *brāhmaṇas*! now I would separately narrate the code of conduct meant for the kings.(31)

इति हारीते धर्मशास्त्रे प्रथमोऽध्यायः।

NOTES

1. Of the four *varṇas* namely *brāhmaṇa, kṣatriya, vaiśya* and *śūdra,* the first three are twice-born (*dvija*), once at their natural birth and again at their initiation when they are invested with the sacred thread and received into Āryan society. The *śūdra* has no initiation and is often not treated as Āryan at all.
2. The *Laghu-Hārīta-smṛti* as available in *Aṣṭādaśa Smṛti* gives here another reading. It is ब्राह्मणेनैव ह्युत्पन्नो।
3. In the *Laghu-Hārīta-Smṛti* appearing in the collection *Smṛti-Sandarbha* Part.II, *Dharmaśāstra-Saṁgraha* (Mahadeva Shastri), *Dharmaśāstra-Saṁgraha* Vol. I (Jīvānanda) and that of Upādhyāya the reading here is वेदवित् but it does not fit into the context.
4. Vaiśvadeva sacrifice-An offering to all deties (*Viśvedevas*) made by presenting oblations to fire before meals. For details see *Manusmṛti* Ch. III 83-86, 108, 121

CHAPTER - II

Duties of three varṇas-*kṣatriya, vaiśya* and *śūdra*

क्षत्रादीनां प्रवक्ष्यामि यथावदनुपूर्वशः।
येषु प्रवृत्ता विधिना सर्वे यान्ति परां गतिम्॥१॥

Now I would narrate in due order the code of conduct of *kṣatriya* and other *varṇas* by following which they all would attain highest bliss.(1)

राज्यस्थः क्षत्रियश्चापि प्रजा धर्मेण पालयन्।
कुर्यादध्ययनं सम्यग् यजेद्यज्ञान् यथाविधि॥२॥

A *kṣatriya* who is in charge of ruling over a kingdom, should righteously protect his subjects. Besides, he should devotedly study the Vedas and duly perform the sacrifices in the manner prescribed by the *Śāstras*.(2)

दद्याद् दानं द्विजातिभ्यो धर्मबुद्धिसमन्वितः।
स्वभार्यानिरतो नित्यं षड्भागार्हः सदा नृपः॥३॥

Well-disposed to virtue and piety he should make gifts to the *brāhmaṇas* and be ever devoted to his legally wedded wife; a king is always entitled to only one sixth part of the income of his subjects.(3)

नीतिशास्त्रार्थकुशलः सन्धिविग्रहतत्त्ववित्।

देवब्राह्मणभक्तश्च पितृकार्यपरस्तथा॥४॥

Versed in the science of politics he is expected to be well-conversant with the principles to be followed for making an alliance (*sandhi*) or for starting a war (*vigraha*); devoted to gods and *brāhmaṇas* he should give utmost attention to offering oblations or performing sacrifices in honour of the deceased ancestors.(4)

धर्मेण यजनं कार्यमधर्मपरिवर्जनम्।

उत्तमां गतिमाप्नोति क्षत्रियोऽप्येवमाचरन्॥५॥

He should perform sacrifices righteously and shun unrighteousness totally. A *kṣatriya* leading his life in this way attains the highest bliss.(5)

गोरक्षां कृषिवाणिज्यं कुर्याद्वैश्यो यथाविधि।

दानं देयं यथाशक्त्या ब्राह्मणानाञ्च भोजनम्॥६॥

As prescribed by the code of conduet a *vaiśya* should engage himself in three professions-maintenance of cattle, agriculture and trade; as far as possible he should feed the *brāhmaṇas* and make gifts to them.(6)

दम्भमोहविनिर्मुक्तस्तथा वागनसूयकः।

स्वदारनिरतो दान्तः परदारविवर्जितः॥७॥

Freed from pride and delusion, he should never give vent to jealous words; devoted to his legally wedded wife the *vaiśya* with his sense-organs under restraint, should have absolutely no relation with another's wife.(7)

धनैर्विप्रान् भोजयित्वा यज्ञकाले तु याजकान्।
अप्रभुत्वञ्च वर्तेत धर्मेष्वादेहपातनात्॥८॥

At the time of sacrifices it behaves a *vaiśya* to feed the priests and please the *brāhmaṇas* with gifts of wealth. In religious rites he should not at all show off his lordship till death.(8)

यज्ञाध्ययनदानानि कुर्यान्नित्यमतन्द्रितः।
पितृकार्यपरश्चैव नरसिंहार्च्चनापरः॥९॥

Everyday he should zealously perform the sacrifices, study the Vedas and bestow gifts (on the suppliants). Devoted to the worship fo Lord Narasiṁha he should also propitiate the deceased ancestors (by offering oblations or performing sacrifices).(9)

एतद्वैश्यस्य धर्मोयं स्वधर्ममनुतिष्ठति।
एतदाचरते यो हि स स्वर्गी नात्र संशयः॥१०॥

This is the code of conduct for a *vaiśya* who remains devoted to his own duties; a *vaiśya* who abides by this code of conduct undoubtedly goes to heaven.(10)

वर्णत्रयस्य शुश्रूषां कुर्याच्छूद्रः प्रयत्नतः।
दासवद् ब्राह्मणानाञ्च विशेषेण समाचरेत्॥११॥

With all care the *śūdra* should serve the three higher *varṇas* and specifically he should serve the *brāhmaṇas* as a slave.(11)

अयाचितप्रदाता च कष्टं वृत्त्यर्थमाचरेत्।
पाकयज्ञविधानेन यजेद्देवमतन्द्रितः॥१२॥

Without being asked for he should make gifts and earn his livelihood through hardship. In keeping with the rules of *pākayajña*[1] he should zealously worship the deity.(12)

शूद्राणामधिकं कुर्यादर्च्चनं न्यायवर्तिनाम्।
धारणं जीर्णवस्त्रस्य विप्रस्योच्छिष्टभोजनम्।
स्वदारेषु रतिश्चैव परदारविवर्जनम्॥१३॥

Being a *śūdra* himself it behoves him to show high regards and respects to the righteous *śūdras*; clothed in rags, he should take the remnants of a *brāhmaṇa's* food. Besides, having absolutely no relation with another's wife, he should amuse himself with his legally wedded wife.(13)

इत्थं कुर्यात् सदा शूद्रो मनोवाक्कायकर्मभिः।
स्थानमैन्द्रमवाप्नोति नष्टपापः सुपुण्यकृत्॥१४॥

With his body, mind and speech a *śūdra* should always undertake to his duties in this manner; having performed righteous deeds he is cleansed of all his sins and after death attains the world of Indra.(14)

वर्णेषु धर्मा विविधामयोक्ता यथा तथा ब्रह्ममुखेरिताः पुरा।
शृणुध्वमत्राश्रमधर्ममाद्यं मयोच्यमानं क्रमशो मुनीन्द्राः॥१५॥

In due order I have narrated the different codes of conduct for the different *varṇas* as in the days of yore it came out of the mouth of Lord Brahmā. O revered sages! now please listen to the code of conduct for the first *āśrama*; I am narrating it one after the other.(15)

इति हारीते धर्मशास्त्रे द्वितीयोऽध्यायः।

NOTE

1. *Pākayajña*—It is a simple domestic sacrifice.

CHAPTER - III

Duties of *brahmacārins*

उपनीतो माणवको[१] वसेद् गुरुकुलेषु च।
गुरोः कुले प्रियं कुर्यात् कर्मणा मनसा गिरा॥१॥

After the '*upanayana*'[2] ceremony is over, the disciple should reside with the preceptor; in thought, speech and deed he should do what is dear to his preceptor.(1)

ब्रह्मचर्य्यमधःशय्या तथा वह्नेरुपासना।
उदकुम्भान् गुरोर्दद्याद् गोग्रासञ्चेन्धनानि च॥२॥
कुर्य्यादध्ययनञ्चैव ब्रह्मचारी यथाविधि।
विधिं त्यक्त्वा प्रकुर्व्वाणो न स्वाध्यायफलं लभेत्॥३॥

Leading the life of a celebrate, the disciple would sleep on the bare ground and worship the Fire; he should devote himself to the service of his preceptor by procuring pitchers of water, grass for cattle and faggots (for performing sacrifices). In keeping with the precepts enjoined upon him, the *brahmacārin* should take lessons on the Vedas; anyone not following the precepts or the prescribed code of conduct is deprived of the religious merit resulting from the study of the Vedas.(2-3)

यः कश्चित् कुरुते धर्मं विधिं हित्वा दुरात्मवान्।
न तत्फलमवाप्नोति कुर्वाणोऽपि विधिच्युतः॥४॥

If a wicked fellow deviating from rules performs virtuous deeds, divested of principles he cannot enjoy the fruits of his actions.(4)

तस्माद्वेदव्रतानीह चरेत् स्वाध्यायसिद्धये।
शौचाचारमशेषं तु शिक्षयेद् गुरुसन्निधौ॥५॥

Therefore for attaining success in his Vedic studies, he should observe the vows as prescribed in the Vedas (such as paying obeisance to the preceptor and worshipping the Fire etc.). Besides, he should imbibe from his teacher all the different rites relating to personal purification.(5)

अजिनं दण्डकाष्ठञ्च मेखलाञ्चोपवीतकम्।
धारयेदप्रमत्तश्च ब्रह्मचारी समाहितः॥६॥

Besides, the *brahmacārin* calm and composed in his mind should punctiliously put on the skin (of a tiger, lion, elephant etc. especially of a black antelope) and without fail putting on the sacred thread, he should use the staff and the girdle.(6)

सायं प्रातश्चरेद्भैक्षं भोज्यार्थं संयतेन्द्रियः।
आचम्य प्रयतो नित्यं च कुर्याद्दन्तधावनम्॥७॥

With his senses under control, for procuring food the *brahmacārin* should beg alms in the morning and the evening; carefully he should perform *ācamana* (sipping of water before and after meals) and brush his teeth regularly before going for begging alms.(7)

छत्रञ्चोपानहञ्चैव गन्धमाल्यादि वर्जयेत्।

नृत्यगीतमथालापं मैथुनञ्च विवर्जयेत्॥८॥

He should abstain from the use of umbrella, sandals, unguents, perfumes and garlands; and more specifically he should avoid dance, music, gossip and copulation.(8)

हस्त्यश्वारोहणञ्चैव संत्यजेत् संयतेन्द्रियः।

सन्ध्योपास्तिं प्रकुर्व्वीत ब्रह्मचारी व्रतस्थितः॥९॥

With his senses under restraint, he should also abstain from riding on the horses and elephants. The *brahmacārin* observing the vows, should duly perform his evening adoration.(9)

अभिवाद्य गुरोः पादौ सन्ध्याकर्मावसानतः।

तथा योगं प्रकुर्व्वीत मातापित्रोश्च भक्तितः॥१०॥

After *sandhyā* rites are over, he should bow down at the feet of his preceptor. And he should devotedly pay obeisance to his parents by mentally remembering them.(10)

एतेषु त्रिषु नष्टेषु नष्टाः स्युः सर्वदेवताः।

एतेषां शासने तिष्ठेद् ब्रह्मचारी विमत्सरः॥११॥

All the gods are displeased if these three (the preceptor, the father and the mother) are displeased. The *brahmacārin* free from pride should abide by their command.(11)

अधीत्य च गुरोर्वेदान् वेदौ वा वेदमेव वा।

गुरवे दक्षिणां दद्यात् संयमी ग्राममावसेत्॥१२॥

After finishing the study of one, two or all the Vedas from the preceptor, he should give to his preceptor whatever the latter asks for; then the self-restrained *brahmacārin* should take up his residence in a village.(12)

यस्यैतानि सुगुप्तानि जिह्वोपस्थोदरं करः।

संन्याससमयं कृत्वा ब्राह्मणो ब्रह्मचर्य्यया॥१३॥

तस्मिन्नेव नयेत् कालमाचार्य्ये यावदायुषम्।

तदभावे च तत्पुत्रे तच्छिष्ये वाथवा कुले॥१४॥

A *brāhmaṇa* whose tongue, appetite, hands and the generative organ are under strict control, may take a pledge of *sannyāsa* and lead his life as a celebate near the same preceptor so long as he lives. In the absence of preceptor he may put up with his son; in the absence of the latter (preceptor's son) he may put up with his disciple; and in case of absence of the disciple he may live with the the family of the preceptor.(13-14)

न विवाहो न संन्यासो नैष्ठिकस्य विधीयते॥१५॥

Neither marriage nor absolute renunciation is laid down for a *naiṣṭhika*[3].(15)

इमं यो विधिमास्थाय त्यजेद्देहमतन्द्रितः।

नेह भूयोऽपि जायेत ब्रह्मचारी दृढव्रतः॥१६॥

Thus the *brahmacārin* of firm vows who zealously

follows this prescribed code of conduct and (in course of time) renounces his body, is not born again in this world.(16)

यो ब्रह्मचारी विधिना समाहितश्चरेत् पृथिव्यां गुरुसेवने रतः।

संप्राप्य विद्यामतिदुर्लभां शिवां फलं च तस्याः सुलभं तु विन्दति॥१७॥

A *brahmacārin* who, conforming to prescribed code of conduct and devoted to the service of his preceptor, moves about on the earth, is blessed to have the rare auspicious knowledge and to get easily the fruits resulting from it.(17)

इति हारीते धर्मशास्त्रे तृतीयोऽध्यायः।

NOTES

1. The reading in the *Laghu-Hārita-Smṛti* appearing in the collection *Smṛti-Sandarbha* Part-II, *Dharmaśāstra-Saṁgraha* (Mahādeva Shastri), *Dharmaśāstra-Saṁgraha* Vol. I (Jīvananda) and that of Upādhayāya is मानवको, but in the other three texts it is माणवको which is lexically correct. This word is constituted of मनु+अण्+(क) which means a boy, a 1ad, a youngster or more popularly a scholar or religious student.

2. *Upanayana*—It is otherwise known as investiture ceremony. In *upanayana* a boy is invested with the sacred thread *(yajñopavita)* which he is supposed to put on continuously from that day forward. The ceremony is confined only to the members of upper three *varṇas* namely the *brāhmaṇa, kṣatriya* and *vaiśya.* The *śūdras*

and lower orders cannot undergo it and they are also not allowed to study or hear the sacred scriptures. Normally initiation is confined to the boys though the girls were sometimes initiated in the Vedic period.

3. A perpetual *brahmacārin* who, with life-long practice of restraint and abstinence, is able to continue with his spiritual preceptor even after his prescribed period is over, is rightly called a *naiṣṭhika.*

CHAPTER - IV

Duties of house-holders

गृहीतवेदाध्ययनः श्रुतशास्त्रार्थतत्त्ववित्।

असमानार्षगोत्रां हि कन्यां सभ्रातृकां शुभाम्॥१॥

सर्व्वावयवसंपूर्णां सुवृत्तामुद्वहेन्नरः।

ब्राह्मेण विधिना कुर्य्यात् प्रशस्तेन द्विजोत्तमः॥२॥

तथान्ये बहवः प्रोक्ता विवाहा वर्णधर्म्मतः॥३क॥

After completing the study of the Vedas, a person proficient in meaning and essence of the Vedas and other related scriptures, should marry a bride who must not have the same *gotra*[1] or the same *pravara*[2], who must have a brother, who has limbs void of any defect and who is endowed with beauty, conduct and character. It is a very much necessary that the best of twice-born should get married in accordance with the celebrated *Brāhma*[3] form of marriage. Various other forms of marriage also have been spoken of in keeping with the duties of different *varṇas*.(1-3a)

उपासनञ्च विधिवदाहृत्य द्विजपुङ्गवाः॥३ख॥

सायं प्रातश्च जुहुयात् सर्वकालमतन्द्रितः।

स्नानं कार्य्यं ततोनित्यं दन्तधावनपूर्व्वकम्॥४॥

O foremost twice-born ones! it behoves a person to duly collect the sacrificial materials and to zealously offer oblations (to the fire) everyday in the morning and in the evening. After brushing the teeth regularly he should then take his bath.(3b-4)

उषःकाले समुत्थाय कृतशौचो यथाविधि।

मुखे पर्य्युषिते नित्यं भवत्यप्रयतो नरः॥५॥

Early in the morning he should leave his bed and duly perform purificatory rites. The mouth remaining stale because of sleeping for the whole night, one loses control over oneself.(5)

तस्माच्छुष्कमथार्द्रं वा भक्षयेद्दन्तकाष्ठकम्।

करञ्जं खादिरं वापि कदम्बं कुरवं तथा॥६॥

सप्तपर्णपृश्निपर्णीजम्वुनिम्बं तथैव च।

अपामार्गञ्च बिल्वञ्चार्कञ्चोदुम्बरमेव च॥७॥

एते प्रशस्ताः कथिता दन्तधावनकर्म्मणि।

दन्तकाष्ठस्य भक्षश्च समासेन प्रकीर्त्तितः॥८॥

Hence one should use tooth-stick either wet or dry. Karañja, Khadira, Kadamba, Kurava, Saptaparṇa, Pṛśniparṇī, Jambu, Nimba, Apāmārga, Bilva, Arka, Udumbara—for brushing the teeth the twings of the aforesaid trees are highly spoken of. Thus the use of tooth-sticks has been narrated briefly.(6-8)

सर्वे कण्टकिनः पुण्याः क्षीरिणश्च यशस्विनः।

अष्टाङ्गुलेन मानेन दन्तकाष्ठमिहोच्यते।

प्रादेशमात्रमथवा तेन दन्तान् विशोधयेत्॥९॥

All thorny twigs endow a person with religious merit; milky ones bring fame to a person. The twig to be used as tooth-brush is supposed to be of the measure of eight fingers (*aṅgulas*). Or else one may brush one's teeth with a twig of the size of a span measured from the tip of the thumb to that of the forefinger (a measure of twelve *aṅgulas*).(9)

प्रतिपत्पर्वषष्ठीषु नवम्याञ्चैव सत्तमाः।

दन्तानां काष्ठसंयोगाद्दहत्यासप्तमं कुलम्॥१०॥

But O most righteous ones! on first lunar days, *parva*[4] days such as the eighth and fourteenth day of each fortnight, new moon, full moon, the entrance of the sun into a new sign (*saṁkrānti*) and moreover on sixth and ninth lunar days if one uses the twigs of the aforesaid trees, one ruins one's ancestors for seven generations.(10)

अभावे दन्तकाष्ठानां प्रतिषिद्धदिनेषु च।

अपां द्वादशगण्डूषैर्मुखशुद्धिं समाचरेत्॥११॥

On the days a twig is not available or on the days interdicted for brushing the teeth, one should cleanse one's mouth by rinsing with twelve handfuls of water.(11)

स्नात्वा मन्त्रवदाचम्य पुनराचमनं चरेत्।

मन्त्रवत् प्रोक्ष्य चात्मानं प्रक्षिपेदुदकाञ्जलिम्॥१२॥

After brushing the teeth one should bathe. Then having rinsed the mouth in course of reciting the *mantras*, one should again rinse it. Thereafter sprinkling one's self with water while reciting the *mantras*, one should offer handfuls of water to the sun-god.(12)

आदित्येन सह प्रातर्मन्देहा नाम राक्षसाः।
युद्ध्यन्ति वरदानेन ब्रह्मणोऽव्यक्तजन्मनः॥१३॥
उदकाञ्जलिनिःक्षेपा गायत्र्या चाभिमन्त्रिताः।
निघ्नन्ति राक्षसान् सर्वान् मन्देहाख्यान् द्विजेरिताः॥१४॥
ततः प्रयाति सविता ब्राह्मणैरभिरक्षितः।
मरीच्याद्यैर्महाभागैः सनकाद्यैश्च योगिभिः॥१५॥
तस्मान्न लङ्घयेत् सन्ध्यां सायं प्रातः समाहितः।
उल्लङ्घयति यो मोहात् स याति नरकं ध्रुवम्॥१६॥

By virtue of the boon conferred by Brahmā of unmanifested birth, the demons called 'Mandehas'[5] fight every morning with the sun-god, but when in honour of the sun-god the *brāhmaṇas* offer handfuls of water consecrated with the Gāyatrī *mantra*, all the demons—the 'Mandehas' are destroyed. Thus protected by illustrious *brāhmaṇas* like Marīci and others and the ascetics like Sanaka etc., the sun-god (*Savitṛ*) proceeds in the sky. Therefore one, calm and composed (*samāhitaḥ*) should never ignore *sandhyā* both in morning and the evening. Any one, who through ignorance fails to perform *sandhyā*, is sure to go to hell.(13-16)

सायं मन्त्रवदाचम्य प्रोक्ष्य सूर्य्यस्य चाञ्जलिम्।
दत्त्वा प्रदक्षिणं कुर्य्याज्जलं स्पृष्ट्वा विशुद्ध्यति॥१७॥

Once again in the evening having rinsed one's mouth in course of reciting the *mantras* one sprinkles one's own self with water and offers handfuls of water in honour of the sun-god. Next one should perform the rite of circumambulation; then by touching the water one is purified.(17)

पूर्व्वां सन्ध्यां सनक्षत्रामुपासीत यथाविधि।
गायत्रीमभ्यसेत्तावद् यावदादित्यदर्शनात्॥१८॥

In the morning when the stars are visible, in the prescribed manner one should start performing *sandhya* and should continue reciting the Gāyatrī *mantra* till the sun is visible in the east.(18)

उपास्य पश्चिमां सन्ध्यां सादित्याञ्च यथाविधि।
गायत्रीमभ्यसेत्तावद्यावत्तारा न पश्यति॥१९॥

In the evening when the sun is visible in the sky, in the prescribed manner one should go on performing *sandhyā* and should continue reciting the Gāyatrī as long as the stars are not visible.(19)

ततश्चावसथं प्राप्य कृत्वा होमं स्वयं बुधः।
सञ्चिन्त्य पोष्यवर्गस्य भरणार्थं विचक्षणः॥२०॥

Thereafter on returning to his residence the learned twice-born should offer oblations in the fire and with foresight he should think of the measures to be taken for supporting his dependants.(20)

ततः शिष्यहितार्थाय स्वाध्यायं किञ्चिदाचरेत्।
ईश्वरञ्चैव कार्य्यार्थमभिगच्छेद्द्विजोत्तोमः॥२१॥

Then for the good of his disciples for sometime he should devote himself to the study of the Vedas. It is desirable that for any act or deed a learned twice-born should submit himself to the Lord.(21)

कुशपुष्पेन्धनादीनि गत्वा दूरं समाहरेत्।

ततो माध्याह्निकं कुर्य्याच्छुचौ देशे मनोरमे॥२२॥

विधिं तस्य प्रवक्ष्यामि समासात् पापनाशनम्।

स्नात्वा येन विधानेन मुच्यते सर्वकिल्विषात्॥२३॥

Repairing to a distant place, he shoud procure kuśa-grass, flowers and sacrificial faggots; then in a sanctified place he should perform the *sandhyā* rites for the mid-day. Now I would tell you, in brief, the prescribed rules relating to the bath by taking which a person is cleansed of all sins.(22-23)

स्नानार्थं मृदमानीय शुद्धाक्षततिलैः सह।

सुमनाश्च ततो गच्छेन्नदीं शुद्धजलाधिकाम्॥२४॥

नद्यां तु विद्यमानायां न स्नायादन्यवारिणि।

न स्नायादल्पतोयेषु विद्यमाने बहूदके॥२५॥

Having procured the materials like lose earth, unbroken white rice and pure sesamum required for the bath, with pleasure and delight one should repair to a river containing sufficient clean water. In case there flows a river nearby, one should avoid taking bath in the water of other places. When water in plenty is available, one need not take one's bath in pools or ponds having insufficient water.(24-25)

सरिद्वरं नदीस्नानं प्रतिस्त्रोतःस्थितश्चरेत्।

तडागादिषु तोयेषु स्नायाच्च तदभावतः॥२६॥

Bath in a river is the best (i.e. conductive to health). One should take one's bath in a river, standing against the current. In the absence of it, one should bathe in the water of a tank or other pools.(26)

शुचिदेशं समभ्युक्ष्य स्थापयेत् सकलाम्बरम्।

मृत्तोयेन स्वकं देहं लिम्पेत् प्रक्षाल्य यत्नतः॥२७॥

स्नानादिकञ्च संप्राप्य कुर्य्यादाचमनं बुधः।

सोऽन्तर्जलं प्रविश्याथ वाग्यतो नियमेन हि।

हरिं संस्मृत्य मनसा मज्जयेच्चोरुमज्जले॥२८॥

Before taking his bath he should put all his cloths in a place sanctified by sprinkling of water. Then rubbing his own body with water and loose earth, the wise one should remove the dirt with care and rinse his mouth. Then entering deep into the water, observing complete silence he should mentally think of (Lord) Hari and dive in thigh-deep water.(27-28)

ततस्तीरं समासाद्य आचम्यापः समन्त्रतः।

प्रोक्षयेद्वारुणैर्मन्त्रैः पावमानीभिरेव च॥२९॥

Then coming over to the bank, he is to rinse his mouth to the accompaniment of the recitation of *mantras*. Next he should sprinkle his body by chanting the *pavamāna* hymns and the hymns dear to Varuṇa.(29)

कुशाग्रकृततोयेन प्रोक्ष्यात्मानं प्रयत्नतः।
स्योनापृथ्वीति मृद्गात्रे इदं विष्णुरिति द्विजाः॥३०॥

Then having carefully sprinkled his own person with water taken by the tips of *kuśa*-grass, O twice-born ones! he should apply loose earth to his body by chanting the *mantra* either "*syonā pṛthvi*" or "*Idam Vīṣṇuḥ*" (Ṛgveda I.22.17=*Śukla Yajurveda* 5.15).(30)

ततो नारायण देवं संस्मरेत् प्रतिमज्जनम्।
निमज्यान्तर्जले सम्यक् क्रियते चाघमर्षणम्॥३१॥

Thereafter in course of diving into the water each time he should mentally think of Lord Nārāyaṇa; then while still plunged in water he should recite the Aghamarṣaṇa hymn (Ṛgveda X.190.1-3).(31)

स्नात्वाक्षततिलैस्तद्वद्देवर्षिपितृभिः सह।
तर्पयित्वा जलं तस्मान्निष्पीड्य च समाहितः॥३२॥
जलतीरं समासाद्य तत्र शुक्ले च वाससी।
परिधायोत्तरीयञ्च कुर्य्यात् केशान्न धूनयेत्॥३३॥

After bath, with unbroken white rice and sesamum he should, as usual, offer oblations of water to the gods, sages and manes. With the offering of oblations of water over, the person, calm and composed is to press out the water from his cloth and reach the bank where he puts on two pieces of white cloth-one for the lower part of the body and the other for covering the upper part. And he is not supposed to shake his hairs (for getting rid of the water).(32-33)

न रक्तमुल्वणं वासो न नीलञ्च प्रशस्यते।

मलाक्तं गन्धहीनञ्च वर्जयेदम्बरं बुधः॥३४॥

With regard to the colour, pieces of cloth of extreme red or dark -blue are not highly spoken of. It behoves a wise and learned person to avoid dirty cloths or the cloths that do not emit good smell.(34)

ततः प्रक्षालयेत् पादौ मृत्तोयेने विचक्षणः।

दक्षिणन्तु करं कृत्वा गोकर्णाकृतिवत् पुनः॥३५॥

त्रिः पिबेदीक्षितं तोयमास्यं द्विः परिमार्जयेत्।

पादौ शिरस्ततोऽभ्युक्ष्य त्रिभिरास्यमुपस्पृशेत्॥३६॥

Then the wise and intelligent person should clean his feet with loose earth and water. Again having converted his right palm into the shape of cow's ear, he should see the (consecrated) water inside, sip it thrice and rinse his mouth twice. Then having sprinkled water both on the head and feet, he should touch his mouth with three fingers.(35-36)

अङ्गुष्ठानामिकाभ्याञ्च चक्षुषी समुपस्पृशेत्।

तथैव पञ्चभिर्मूर्द्ध्नि स्पृशेदेवं समाहितः॥३७॥

With thumb (*aṅguṣṭha*) and the ring finger *anāmikā* he should touch both his eyes; then it is desirable that the calm and composed should touch his head with five fingers.(37)

अनेन विधिनाचम्य ब्राह्मणः शुद्धमानसः।

कुर्व्वीत दर्भपाणिस्तूदङ्मुखः प्राङ्मुखोऽपि वा॥३८॥

प्राणायामत्रयं धीमान् यथान्यायमतन्द्रितः।

जपयज्ञं ततः कुर्य्याद् गायत्रीं वेदमातरम्॥३९॥

Having performed the *ācamana* in this prescribed manner, the pure-minded *brāhmaṇa* should take up the *kuśa*-grass in his hands; facing either north or east the wise and intelligent person, without giving himself to stupor, should duly practise *prāṇāyāma* thrice and thereafter perform the sacrifice of recitation (*japayajña*) of Gāyatrī, the mother of the Vedas.(38-39)

त्रिविधो जपयज्ञः स्यात्तस्य तत्त्वं निबोधत।

वाचिकश्च उपांशुश्च मानसश्च त्रिधाकृतिः॥४०॥

त्रयाणामपि यज्ञानां श्रेष्ठः स्यादुत्तरोत्तरः॥४१॥

There are three varieties of *japayajña* (recitation of Gāyatri)—(1) audibly uttered (*vācika*), (ii) inaudibly uttered (upāṁśu) and (iii) mentally revolved (mānasa); of these three varieties of *japayajña* each succeeding one is more efficacious than the preceeding one; now listen to the peculiarities of each of them.(40-41)

यदुच्चनीचोच्चरितैः शब्दैः स्पष्टपदाक्षरैः।

मन्त्रमुच्चारयन् वाचा जपयज्ञस्तु वाचिकः॥४२॥

The *japayajña* is called *vācika* when the (Gāyatrī)

mantra is recited with its various parts and letters distinctly expressed either in high or low pitch.(42)

शनैरुच्चारयन्मन्त्रं किञ्चिदोष्ठौ प्रचालयेत्।

किञ्चिच्छ्रवणयोग्यः स्यात् स उपांशुः जपः स्मृतः॥४३॥

The *japayajña* is called *upāṁśu* when the (Gāyatrī) *mantra* is recited in a low voice with slight movement of lips and the sound being slightly audible only to the reciter.(43)

धिया पदाक्षरश्रेण्या अवर्णमपदाक्षरम्।

शब्दार्थचिन्तनाभ्यान्तु तदुक्तं मानसं स्मृतम्॥४४॥

The *japayajña* is called *mānasa* when each word and letter of the *mantra* is comprehended by the intellect and the meaning of the words is meditated upon, though the words and letters are not audible.(44)

जपेन देवता नित्यं स्तूयमाना प्रसीदति।

प्रसन्ने विपुलान् गोत्रान् प्राप्नुवन्ति मनीषिणः॥४५॥

The divinity eulogised by the daily recitation of hymns of praise is propitiated. And only at the pleasure (of the divinity), the wise and learned are blessed with offsprings and their race is perpetuated.(45)

राक्षसाश्च पिशाचाश्च महासर्पाश्च भीषणाः।

जपितान्नोपसर्पन्ति दूरादेव प्रयान्ति ते॥४६॥

The demons (*rākṣasas*), the malevolent beings (*piśācas*) and the ferocious huge serpents dare not approach the persons reciting the *mantra* and from a distance they flee away from them.(46)

छन्द ऋष्यादि विज्ञाय जपेन्मन्त्रमतन्द्रितः।
जपेदहरहर्ज्ञात्वा गायत्रीं मनसा द्विजः॥४७॥

It is desirable that one should zealously recite the *mantra* with the knowledge of metre, *rṣi* (the seer who has composed the particular *mantra* or hymn) and other things. And a twice-born should day and night keep on reciting Gāyatrī by constantly meditating upon it.(47)

सहस्त्रपरमां देवीं शतमध्यां दशावराम्।
गायत्रीं यो जपेन्नित्यं स न पापेन लिप्यते॥४८॥

A person used to daily recitation of this Gāyatrī at best for thousand times or for a hundred times or at least for ten times is not sullied by sin.(48)

अथ पुष्पाञ्जलिं कृत्वा भानवे चोर्ध्वबाहुकः।
उदुत्यञ्च जपेत् सूक्तं तच्चक्षुरिति चापरम्॥४९॥

Then offering handfuls of flower in honour of the sun-god with his arms raised up, he should recite the hymn namely *Oṁ udutyam jātavedasam* (*Śukla Yajurveda*-7.41) and another hymn called *Oṁ tat cakṣur devahitam* (*Śukla Yajurveda*-36.24).(49)

प्रदक्षिणमुपावृत्त्य नमस्कुर्य्याद्दिवाकरम्।
ततस्तीर्थेन देवादीनद्भिः सन्तर्पयेद् द्विजः॥५०॥

Performing the rite of circumambulation he would bow down to the sun-god; then the twice-born is supposed to propitiate different deities and manes etc. with the water of the holy places.(50)

स्नानवस्त्रन्तु निष्पीड्य पुनराचमनं चरेत्।

तद्भद्भक्तजनस्येह स्नानं दानं प्रकीर्तितम्॥५१॥

Pressing water out of the cloth used while bathing he should rinse his mouth again. Bathing and making gifts by a devout follower has been thus spoken of here.(51)

दर्भासीनो दर्भपाणिर्ब्रह्मयज्ञविधानतः।

प्राङ्मुखो ब्रह्मयज्ञं तु कुर्याच्छ्रद्धासमन्वितः॥५२॥

ततोऽर्घ्यं भानवे दद्यात्तिलपुष्पाक्षतान्वितम्॥५३क।

Seated on a mat of *kuśa*-grass with *kuśa*-grass in his hands and with his face directed to the east, he devotedly performs the *Brahma-yajña* (study of one's own Veda) according to the prescribed rites and makes an offering of sesamum, flowers and unbroken white rice in honour of the sun-god.(52-53a)

उत्थाय मूर्द्धपर्यन्तं हंसः शुचिषदित्यृचा॥५३ख।

ततो देवं नमस्कृत्य गृहं गच्छेत्ततः पुनः।

विधिना पुरुषसूक्तस्य गत्वा विष्णुं समर्चयेत्॥५४॥

वैश्वदेवं ततः कुर्याद्बलिकर्मविधानतः॥५५क।

Then raising his palms upto his head and reciting the Ṛgvedic hymn *haṁsaḥ śucisat* he should bow down to the sun-god and return home. On reaching home he is supposed to adore Viṣṇu in the prescribed manner by the recita-tion of *Puruṣasūkta*. The next part of his duty is to make proper offerings in honour of all the gods (Viśvedevas).(53b-55a)

गोदोहमात्रमकाङ्क्षेदतिथिं प्रति वै गृही।।५५ख।

अदृष्टपूर्वमज्ञातमतिथिं प्राप्तमर्चयेत्।

स्वागतासनदानेन प्रत्युत्थानेन चाम्बुना।।५६।।

(After having pleased and propitiated the gods, the seers and the manes), for receiving the guests the house-holder waits for as much time as would be required for milking a cow[6]. On the arrival of a guest whom he has neither seen or known before, it is desirable for a house-holder to welcome him by rising up (from the seat) or by making an offer of a seat or water.(55b-56)

स्वागतेनाग्नयस्तुष्टा भवन्ति गृहमेधिनः।

आसनेन तु दत्तेन प्रीतो भवति देवराट्।।५७।।

पादशौचेन पितरः प्रीतिमायान्ति दुर्लभाम्।

अन्नदानेन युक्तेन तृप्यते हि प्रजापतिः।।५८।।

All the three Fires (Gārhapatya, Āhavanīya and Dakṣina) are pleased with the house-holder who welcomes his guests. Indra, the Lord of gods, is pleased when the house-holder offers a seat to the guest; by cleaning the feet of the guest the deceased ancestors get rare pleasure and happiness. And Lord Prajāpati is pleased when food is offered to the guest.(57-58)

तस्मादतिथये कार्यं पूजनं गृहमेधिना।

भक्त्या च शक्तितो नित्यं विष्णोरर्च्चादनन्तरम्[७]।।५९।।

Therefore everyday after the adoration of Viṣṇu with devotion, it behoves a house-holder to treat the guest with all honour according to his might.(59)

भिक्षाञ्च भिक्षवे दद्यात् परिव्राड्ब्रह्मचारिणे।

अकल्पितान्नादुद्धृत्य सव्यञ्जनसमन्विताम्।।६०।।

He should offer to the ascetic and wandering *brahmacārin*[8] alms consisting of some boiled rice with condiments from the food already prepared.(60)

अकृते वैश्वदेवेऽपि भिक्षौ च गृहमागते।

उद्धृत्य वैश्वदेवार्थं भिक्षां दत्त्वा विसर्जयेत्।।६१।।

In case an ascetic arrives at a house before the Vaiśvadeva offering is performed, setting apart a portion for the Vaiśvadeva offering, the house-holder is supposed to dismiss the ascetic after feeding him.(61)

वैश्वदेवाकृतान् दोषाञ्छक्तो भिक्षुर्व्यपोहितुम्।

नहि भिक्षुकृतान् दोषान् वैश्वदेवो व्यपोहति।।६२।।

Such an ascetic is capable of removing the blemish of not making the Vaiśvadeva offering, but on the contrary the Viśvedevas is incapable of removing the blemish of not feeding an ascetic.(62)

तस्मात् प्राप्ताय यतये भिक्षां दद्यात् समाहितः।

विष्णुरेव यतिच्छाय इति निश्चित्य भावयेत्।।६३।।

Therefore on the arrival of an ascetic, a calm and composed person should offer him alms. It is pertinent for him to regard the ascetic as a replica of Viṣṇu.(63)

सुवासिनीं कुमारीञ्च भोजयित्वा नरानपि।
बालवृद्धांस्ततः शेषं स्वयं भुञ्जीत वा गृही॥६४॥

Only after feeding the young girl, newly-married woman, children and the old people, the house-holder is supposed to partake of the food that is left over.(64)

प्राङ्मुखोदङ्मुखो वापि मौनी च मितभाषर्कः।
अन्नमादौ नमस्कृत्य प्रहृष्टेनान्तरात्मना॥६५॥
एवं प्राणाहुतिं कुर्यान्मन्त्रेण च पृथक् पृथक्।
ततः स्वादुकरान्नञ्च भुञ्जीत सुसमाहितः॥६६॥

While taking food seated facing east or the north, one should observe silence or at least should restrain one's speech. With delighted heart first one should bow to the food; then by reciting different *mantras* in honour of the *prāṇa*, in a calm and composed state one should begin taking the delicious food.(65-66)

आचम्य देवतामिष्टां संस्मरन्नुदरं स्पृशेत्॥
इतिहासपुराणाभ्यां कञ्चित् कालं नयेद् बुधः॥६७॥

After taking the food the prudent house-holder shoulder rinse his mouth; then remembering his tutelary deity he should touch his stomach. Next he would spend sometime in the study of *Itihāsa* and *Purāṇa*.(67)

ततः सन्ध्यामुपासीत बहिर्गत्वा विधानतः।
कृतहोमस्तु भुञ्जीत रात्रौ चातिथिभोजनम्॥६८॥

Then at the approach of the evening he would go

out (to the bank of a lake or river) and perform *sandhyā* in the prescribed manner. Again at night after offering oblations to the Fire and feeding the guests, he would take his food.(68)

सायं प्रातर्द्विजातीनामशनं श्रुतिचोदितम्।
नान्तरा भोजनं कुर्यादग्निहोत्रसमो विधिः॥६९॥

As per the injunctions of the Vedas a twice-born should take ony two meals a day—in the morning and in the evening, and no food in between. This rule of taking meals two times a day is in conformity with the perfomance of *Agnihotra* twice a day in the morning and the evening.(69)

शिष्यानध्यापयेच्चापि अनध्याये विसर्जयेत्।
स्मृत्युक्तानखिलांश्चापि पुराणोक्तानपि द्विजः॥७०॥

Besides the twice-born should teach the Vedas to the disciples, but he should desist from teaching on the days Vedic studies are prohibited (*anadhyāya*). All the days ear-marked for cessation of Vedic study have been referred to in *Smṛtis* and *Purāṇa*-texts.(70)

महानवम्यां द्वादश्यां भरण्यामपि पर्वसु।
तथाक्षयतृतीयायां शिष्यान्नाध्यापयेद् द्विजः॥७१॥
माघमासे तु सप्तम्यां रथ्याख्यायां तु वर्जयेत्।
अध्यापनं समभ्यञ्जन् स्नानकाले च वर्जयेत्॥७२॥
नीयमानं शवं दृष्ट्वा महीस्थं वा द्विजोत्तमाः।
न पठेद्रुदितं श्रुत्वा सन्ध्यायां तु द्विजोत्तमः॥७३॥

A twice-born should refrain from imparting lessons on the following days—*Mahānavamī* (the ninth day of the bright half of Āśvina famous for the worship of goddess Durgā)—the twelfth day (of the bright half of Āśvina), *Bharaṇi* (the *tithi* when the moon is in Bharaṇi *nakṣatra* after Bhādrapada full moon), the *parva* days (the eighth and fourteenth day of each fortnight, new moon, full moon and *saṁkrānti*), *Akṣaya tṛtīyā* (the third day of bright half of Vaiśākha), the seventh day (of the bright half of Māgha) and *Rathyā saptamī*. Likewise there should be no teaching of Vedas when anointed with oil one is taking bath; when one witnesses a deadbody lying on the ground or it is being carried away to the cremation ground. A wise twice-born should also avoid study if he comes across somebody weeping in the evening.(71-73)

दानानि च प्रदेयानि गृहस्थेन द्विजोत्तमाः।

हिरण्यदानं गोदानं पृथिवीदानमेव च॥७४॥

O revered twice-born ones! it is desirable for a householder to bestow gifts of gold, cows or land.(74)

एवं[१०] धर्मो गृहस्थस्य सारभूत[११] उदाहृतः।

य एवं श्रद्धया कुर्यात् स याति ब्रह्मणः पदम्॥७५॥

ज्ञानोत्कर्षश्च तस्य स्यान्नारसिंहप्रसादतः।

तस्मान्मुक्तिमवाप्नोति ब्राह्मणो द्विजसत्तमाः॥७६॥

Thus the essential duties of a house-holder have been narrated (by me). He who performs it with faith and devotion, attains the world of Brahmā. Moreover, with the blessing of Lord Narasiṁha he acquires the highest wisdom and the *brāhmaṇa* gets liberated (from the fetters of *saṁsāra*).(75-76)

एवं हि विप्राः! कथितो मया वः,
समासतः शाश्वतधर्मराशिः।
गृही गृहस्थस्य सतो हि धर्मं
कुर्वन् प्रयत्नाद्धरिमेति युक्तम्॥७७॥

O sages! thus I have narrated to you in brief the eternal code of conduct. A house-holder punctiliously following the code of conduct meant for him goes to Lord Hari and is merged in Him.(77)

इति हारीते धर्मशास्त्रे चतुर्थोऽध्यायः।

NOTES

1-2. *Gotra* and *pravara*—In "*The wonder that was India*" (pp. 154-156) Basham has clearly explained these two words. According to him, *gotra* was "primarily a brāhmanic institution, adopted rather half heartedly by other twice-born classes and hardly affecting the lower orders. All the *brāhmaṇas* were believed to have descended from one of the *ṛṣis* or legendary seers, after whom the *gotras* were named. The religious literature generally speaks of seven or eight primeval *gotras,* those of Kāśyapa, Vasiṣṭha, Bhṛgu, Gautama, Bharadvāja, Atri and Viśvāmitra. The eighth *gotra,* that of Agastya, is named after the sage who is said to have taken the Vedic religion beyond the Vindhyas". These primeval *gotras* are multiplied in the later period by including the names of many other ancient sages. This *gotra* bears its importance in connection with marriage which is generally forbidden to persons of equal *gotra.*

It is *pravara* which makes the position further complicated. In the daily worship the *brāhmaṇa* mentions not only the name of the founder of his *gotra* but also the names of some other sages who are believed to be the remote ancestors of his family. The formula generally contains three or five names and in fact it stands as a further bar to marriage, for the same names might be there in the *pravaras* of families of other *gotras.* According to the tradition, marriage is impossible with a member of another *gotra* having one *pravara* name in common. Thus to put it briefly, marriage is totally interdicted within the same *gotra* or same *pravara.*

3. Of the eight types of marriage *Brāhma* form of marriage is the first and foremost one in which the bridegroom, being invited by the father-in-law, proceeds to his house in the company of friends and relatives and he gets married there to a bride of the same class in accordance with the prescribed rites. The other seven types of marriage are-*Daiva, Ārṣa, Prājāpatya, Gāndharva, Āsura, Rākṣasa* and *Paiśāca,* of which the last one is the worst. All these eight types of marriage are referred to in the *Viṣṇu Purāṇa* (III Ch. 10.24) as follows:—

   ब्राह्मदैवतथैवार्षः प्राजापत्यस्तथासुरः।

   गान्धर्वराक्षसौ चान्यौ पैशाचश्चाष्टमोऽधमः।।

   Cf. *Manusmriti* Ch. III. 21; 27-34. See also Basham A.L.— *The wonder that was India* p. 169.

4. The redactor of *Viṣṇu Purāṇa* has clearly explained the word *parva* in the following verse :

   चतुर्दश्यष्टमीचैव अमावास्याथपूर्णिमा।

पर्वाण्येतानि राजेन्द्र! रविसंक्रान्तिरेव च।। *Viṣṇu Purāṇa,* III.Ch. 11. 115.

5. The fearful demons called 'Mandehas' are the enemies of sun-god. Due to curse of Brahmā they die daily though their bodies never perish. At the approach of evening they always devour the sun-god, but early in the morning when the pious *brāhmaṇas* offer water purified with *Oṁkāra* and consecrated by Gāyatrī, the foul demons are destroyed. *Oṁkāra* represents Viṣṇu, the essence of three Vedas and by its enunciation those demons are killed. With the first oblation offered in the morning rite, free from the clutches of 'Mandehas', the thousand-rayed sun-god shines with all splendour and effulgence and moves ahead in the sky. Therefore performance of *sandhyā* should not be neglected, for he, who neglects it, is said to be guilty of the murder of the sun.
   Vāyu Purāṇa -I. Ch. 50, 162-167.
   Brahmāṇḍa Purāṇa-I.2.Anusaṅgapāda Ch. 21.
   Viṣṇu Purāṇa-II. Ch. 8, 50-59.
6. The other interpretation is that for receiving the guests the house-holder waits till the time of milking the cows.
7. The *Laghu-Hārīta-Smṛti* appearing in the *Aṣṭādaśa Smṛti* has a different reading here. It is पूजयेद्विष्णुमन्वहम्।
8. Vide the *Laws of Manu* S.B.E. Vol. XXV p. 92 comment on III.94.
9. The *Laghu-Hārīta-Smṛti* appearing in the *Aṣṭādaśa Smṛti* mentions this word as मितभाषणः।
10. In the *Laghu-Hārīta-Smṛti* appearing in the *Aṣṭādaśa Smṛti* the reading here is एष.
11. In the *Laghu-Hārīta-Smṛti* appearing in the *Dharmaśāstra-Saṁgraha* (Mahadeva Shastri) and *Dharmaśāstra-Saṁgraha* Vol. I (Upādhayāya) the reading सायं श्रूत makes

no sense. So also the reading सायंभूत noticed respectively in the *Laghu-Hārīta-Smṛti* of *Smṛti-Sandarbha* Part-II and *Dharmaśāstra-Saṁgraha* Vol. I (Jīvānanda) is unmeaningful. However, we meet with the correct reading सारभूत in the three other texts.

CHAPTER - V

Duties of *vānaprasthas*

अतः परं प्रवक्ष्यामि वानप्रस्थस्य सत्तमाः!।

धर्माश्रमं महाभागाः! कथ्यमानं निबोधत॥१॥

O most righteous ones! hereafter I would narrate the code of conduct relating to the stage of life of a *vānaprastha* (forest-hermit). O revered sages! please listen to it.(1)

गृहस्थः पुत्रपौत्रादीन् दृष्ट्वा पलितमात्मनः।

भार्य्यां पुत्रेषु निःक्षिप्य सह वा प्रविशेद्वनम्॥२॥

At the approach of old age (notcing his skin to be wrinkled and the hairs turning white) a house-holder blessed with sons and grand-sons should entrust his wife to the care of his sons and betake himself to the forest alone. Or else in the company of his wife he may repair to the forest.(2)

नखरोमाणि च तथा सितगात्रत्वगादि च।

धारयन् जुहुयादग्निं वनस्थो विधिमाश्रितः॥३॥

With nails and hairs growing on the body and white skin covering the body a hermit, living in a forest should offer oblations to the sacred fire as enjoined by the scriptures.(3)

धान्यैश्च वनसंभूतैर्नीवाराद्यैरनिन्दितैः।
शाकमूलफलैर्वापि कुर्यान्नित्यं प्रयत्नतः॥४॥

The hermit should make it a daily habit of subsisting on paddy and wild grains (*nīvāra*) growing in forest-tracts or he may carefully partake of leaves, roots and fruits.(4)

त्रिकालस्नानयुक्तस्तु कुर्य्यात्तीव्रं तपस्तदा।
पक्षान्ते वा समश्नीयान्मासान्ते वा स्वपक्वभुक्॥५॥

After taking his bath three times a day-morning, noon and evening he should engage himself in austere penance. Having cooked his food himself the forest-hermit may take his meal at the end of a fortnight or a month.(5)

तथा चतुर्थकाले तु भुञ्जीयादष्टमेऽथवा।
षष्ठे च कालेऽप्यथवा वायुभक्षोऽथवा भवेत्॥६॥

Either he may omit three meal times (full one day and the morning of the second) and take his food only in the evening of the second day or he may omit five meal times (full two days and the morning of the third) and take his food only in the evening of the third day or he may omit seven meal times (full three days and the morning of the fourth) and take his food only in the evening of the fourth day. Or else he may subsist only on air.(6)

घर्मे पञ्चाग्निमध्यस्थस्तथा वर्षे निराश्रयः।
हेमन्ते च जले स्थित्वा नयेत् कालं तपश्चरन्॥७॥

In summer he should practise severe austerities by standing in the midst of five fires (four fires in the four directions and the blazing sun overhead); in the rains he should remain standing in the open without any shelter and in the winter he should practise penance by standing in the midst of water.(7)

एवञ्च कुर्वता येन कृतबुद्धिर्यथाक्रमम्।

अग्निं स्वात्मनि कृत्वा तु प्रव्रजेदुत्तरां दिशम्॥८॥

आदेहपातं वनगो मौनमास्थाय तापसः।

स्मरन्नतीन्द्रियं ब्रह्म ब्रह्मलोके महीयते॥९॥

Thus through the practice of various penances the man of resolute character should repose the fire in his own mind. Observing complete silence the forest-hermit should proceed in the northern direction and till his death (lit. till the body falls to rise no more) he should engage himself in constant meditaiton of the imperceptible Brahman. And after his death he is adored in the world of Brahmā.(8-9)

तपो हि यः सेवति वन्यवासः

समाधियुक्तः प्रयतान्तरात्मा[१]।

विमुक्तपापो विमलः प्रशान्तः

स याति दिव्यं पुरुषं पुराणम्॥१०॥

The forest-hermit who, with concentration of body and mind, resorts to penance and has his senses both external and internal under restraint, is purged of all sins;

with his heart pure and sublime he goes to the divine abode of the Primordial Being.(10)

इति हारीते धर्मशास्त्रे पंचमोऽध्यायः।

NOTE

1. In the *Laghu-Hārīta-Smṛti* appearing in the collection *Dharmaśāstra-Saṁgraha* (Mahadeva Shastri) and the *Dharmaśāstra-Saṁgraha* Vol.I (Upādhyāya) the reading प्रयतात्तरात्मा is unmeaningful. Another reading प्रयतात्मरात्मा in the *Laghu-Hārīta-Smṛti* of Dharmaśāstra-Saṁgraha Vol. I by Jivānanda also makes no sense. However, the correct reading प्रयतान्तरात्मा is noticed in the rest four texts.

CHAPTER - VI

Duties of Wandering Mendicants (*yati*)

अतः परं प्रवक्ष्यामि चतुर्थाश्रममुत्तमम्।
श्रद्धया तदनुष्ठाय तिष्ठन्मुच्येत बन्धनात्॥१॥

I would hereafter narrate the excellent fourth stage of life (*yati*); by leading that prescribed life with faith and devotion one is released from the fetters (*of saṁsāra*).(1)

एवं वनाश्रमे तिष्ठन् पातयंश्चैव किल्विषम्।
चतुर्थमाश्रमं गच्छेत् संन्यासविधना द्विजः॥२॥

While leading the life of an anchorite (*vanāśrama*) the twice-born (*dvija*) is absolved of sins; then he enters the fourth *āśrama* by renouncing everything.(2)

दत्त्वा पितृभ्यो देवेभ्यो मानुषेभ्यश्च यत्नतः।
दत्त्वा श्राद्धं पितृभ्यश्च मानुषेभ्यस्तथात्मनः॥३॥
इष्टिं वैश्वानरीं कृत्वा प्राङ्मुखोदङ्मुखोऽपि वा।
अग्निं स्वात्मनि संरोप्य मन्त्रवित् प्रव्रजेत् पुनः॥४॥

At first with all care he should make gifts to the gods, ancestors and human beings. Then he should offer *śrāddha* for the ancestors, human relations and his own self. Next facing eastern or northern direction he performs the sacrifice in honour of *Vaiśvānara* (*Vaiśvānareṣṭi*); then the person well-conversant with the *mantras*, should repose the sacred fire in his own self and enter upon the life of a wandering mendicant.(3-4)

ततः प्रभृति पुत्रादौ स्नेहालापादि वर्जयेत्।
बन्धूनामभयं दद्यात् सर्वभूताभयं तथा॥५॥

Since then the mendicant should give up attachment for progeny or any kind of conversation with them. He should give assurance of safety to his kinsmen and all other creatures as well.(5)

त्रिदण्डं वैणवं सम्यक् सन्ततं समपर्वकम्।
वेष्टितं कृष्णगोवालरज्जुमच्चतुरङ्गुलम्॥६॥
शौचार्थं मानसार्थञ्च[१] मुनिभिः समुदाहृतम्॥७क॥

The mendicant should carry three long staves tied together so as to form one; formed of bamboo plant, decent and beautiful, the staves should have the joints at equal distance. For four *aṅgulas* at the top the staves should be tied up with the tail of a black cow. It is duly precribed by the sages for physical and mental purification.(6-7a)

कौपीनाच्छादनं वासः कन्थां शीतनिवारिणीम्॥७ख॥
पादुके चापि गृह्णीयात् कुर्यान्नान्यस्य संग्रहम्।
एतानि तस्य लिङ्गानि यतेः प्रोक्तानि सर्वदा॥८॥
संगृह्य कृतसंन्यासो गत्वा तीर्थमनुत्तमम्।

स्नात्वाचम्य च विधिवद्वस्त्रपूतेन वारिणा॥९॥
तर्पयित्वा तु देवांश्च मन्त्रवद् भास्करं नमेत्।
आत्मनः प्राङ्मुखो मौनी प्राणायामत्रयं चरेत्॥१०॥

A ragged garment (to be worn over the privities), an upper garment (to cover the body), a blanket of thick fabrics for protection from cold and a pair of sandals-these are the only requisites of a mendicant and he should procure nothing more. These are said to be the distinguishing marks of a mendicant who should always procure them. Then the mendicant should proceed to the holiest place of pilgrimage; thereafter taking ablutions and rinsing his mouth in the prescribed manner, with the wet rags on his body he should offer libations of water to the gods and bow down to the Sun by reciting the *mantras*. Moreover, with his face directed to the east he should abstain from speech and practise *prāṇāyāma* (restraining or suspending the breath during mental recitation of the names or attributes of a deity) in three different ways[2].(7b-10)

गायत्रीञ्च यथाशक्ति जप्त्वा ध्यायेत् परं पदम्।
स्थित्यर्थमात्मनो नित्यं भिक्षाटनमथाचरेत्॥११॥

Then having muttered the 'Gāyatrī' *mantra* according to his might, he should meditate on the Supreme Self. (After finishing all his obligatory duties), for his own sustenance everyday he should wander about begging for alms.(11)

सायंकाले तु विप्राणां गृहाण्यभ्यवपद्य तु।
सम्यक् याचेच्च कवलं दक्षिणेन करेण वै॥१२॥

पात्रं वामकरे स्थाप्य दक्षिणेन तु शेषयेत्।
यावतान्नेन तृप्तिः स्यात्तावद्भैक्षं समाचरेत्॥१३॥

It is desirable that in the evening a mendicant should repair to the residence of the *brāhmaṇas* and ask for a morsel of food by extending his right hand. Having taken up the bowl with his left hand he should collect the alms and put them inside the bowl with his right hand; he should beg till he procures food capable of gratifying him (he should not collect alms more than what is necessary for him).(12-13)

ततो निवृत्त्य तत्पात्रं संस्थाप्यान्यत्र संयमी।
चतुर्भिरङ्गुलैश्छाद्य ग्रासमात्रं समाहितः॥१४॥
सर्वव्यञ्जनसंयुक्तं पृथक् पात्रे नियोजयेत्।
सूर्यादिभूतदेवेभ्यो दत्त्वा संप्रोक्ष्य वारिणा॥१५॥
भुञ्जीत पात्रपुटके पात्रे वा वाग्यतो[3] यतिः।
वटकाश्वत्थपर्णेषु कुम्भीतैन्दुकपात्रके॥१६॥
कोविदारकदम्बेषु न भुञ्जीयात् कदाचन॥१७क॥

When he returns from begging, the mendicant with his senses restrained, places the begging bowl at another place, then carefully he takes out a morsel of food mixed with all sorts of curries with his four fingers and puts it in a different vessel; thereafter having sprinkled water over the particular vessel he offers it to the elemental divinities like Sun etc. With his offerings to the divinities over, the mendicant observing complete silence would take the food in a vessel made by either leaves or metal. The leaves which the mendicant uses as his vessel, should never be those of *Vaṭa, Aśvattha, Kumbhī, Tainduka, Kovidāra* or *Kadamba*.(14-17a)

मलाक्ताः सर्वं उच्यन्ते यतयः कांस्यभोजिनः॥१७ख॥

कांस्यभाण्डेषु यत् पाको गृहस्थस्य तथैव च।

कांस्ये भोजयतः सर्वं किल्विषं प्राप्नुयात्तयोः॥१८॥

All the mendicants who are used to take their food in vessels of bell-metal, come to be tarnished (*malāktāḥ*) in due course; a mendicant taking food in vessels of bell-metal is in no way different from a house-holder who cooks his food in vessels of bell-metal. A mendicant taking his food in a vessel of bell-metal partakes of the sins of both—the house-holder (who cooks his food in the vessels of bell-metal) and the person who makes others eat from the same.(17b-18)

भुक्त्वा पात्रे यतिर्नित्यं क्षालयेन्मन्त्रपूर्वकम्।

न दुष्यते च तत्पात्रं यज्ञेषु चमसा इव॥१९॥

After taking food in a vessel of earth or wood, everyday a mendicant is supposed to wash it out with water by reciting the *mantras*. Like vessels used in sacrifices (sacrificial ladles), that earthern or wooden vessel of the mendicant is neverr desecrated.(19)

अथाचम्य निदिध्यास्य उपतिष्ठते भास्करम्।

जपध्यानेतिहासैश्च दिनशेषं नयेद् बुधः॥२०॥

(After taking food and washing out the vessel) the mendicant should rinse his mouth; then resorting to deep meditation he should bow down to the sun-god. (Thus with his daily rites and duties over), the wise mendicant should spend the rest of the day in muttering prayers, in medita-tion and the study of *Itihāsas*.(20)

कृतसन्ध्यस्ततो रात्रिं नयेद्देवगृहादिषु।
हृत्पुण्डरीकनिलये ध्यायेदात्मानमव्ययम्॥२१॥

At the approach of the night he should offer his evening prayers and respose in some temple; then he should meditate upon the imperishable Self seated in the lotus of his heart.(21)

यदि धर्मरतिः शान्तः सर्वभूतसमो वशी।
प्राप्नोति परमं स्थानं यत्प्राप्य न निवर्तते॥२२॥

If a mendicant is calm, self-restrained,greatly attached to religion and above all, impartial to all the creatures, then he attains the highest abode of the Lord whence there is no return.(22)

त्रिदण्डभृद्यो हि पृथक् समाचारेच्छनै शनैर्यस्तु बहिर्मुखक्षैः[४]।
संमुच्य संसारसमस्तबन्धनात् स याति विष्णोरमृतात्मनः
पदम्॥२३॥

The holder of the tripple staff (mendicant) who withdraws his sense-organs already attached to the external objects of sight, smell, taste, touch and sound and thus gradually becomes indifferent, is freed from all the fetters of worldly existence and attains to the exalted nectar-like abode of Lord Viṣṇu.

इति हारीते धर्मशास्त्रे षष्ठोऽध्यायः।

NOTES

1. Only in the *Laghu-Hārīta-Smṛti* appearing in the *Aṣṭādaśa Smṛti* this reading is आसनार्थञ्च but मानसार्थञ्च seems to be the better reading noticed in all other texts.
2. *Prāṇāyāmatraya-Prāṇa yāma* has three components-*pūraka* (inhaling the outside air), *kumbhaka* (keeping in the inhaled air i.e. neither taking in air nor giving it out) and *recaka* (exhaling air from the lungs). Vide Kane, P.V.-*History of Dharmaśāstra* Vol. II, Part-I, p. 317.
3. In all the texts taken up for critical edition, this word has been misspelt as वाचभ्यतो, वावभ्यतो, वावन्यतो etc., but the correct reading is वा वाग्यतो।
4. In the *Laghu-Hārīta-Smṛti* appearing in the collection *Aṣṭādaśa-Smṛti* (pp. 80-113) and the *Smṛti-Sandarbha* Part-II (pp. 974-994) the reading बहिर्मुखाध: makes no sense. The correct reading, however, is बहिर्मुखाक्ष: [बहिर्मुखानि अक्षाणि (इन्द्रियाणि) यस्य, स:] noticed in all other texts.

CHAPTER - VII

Essence of *yoga* Philosophy

वर्णानामाश्रमाणाञ्च कथितं धर्मलक्षणम्।

येन स्वर्गापवर्गञ्च प्राप्नुवन्ति द्विजातयः॥१॥

I have described the code of conduct for various *varṇas* and *āśramas* by observing which the *brāhmaṇas* and people of other castes attain heaven and liberation.(1)

योगशास्त्रं प्रवक्ष्यामि सङ्क्षेपात् सारमुत्तमम्।

यस्य च श्रवणाद्यान्ति मोक्षञ्चैव मुमुक्षवः॥२॥

Now I would briefly narrate the essence of *Yoga* philosophy by listening to which people desirous of liberation attain it.(2)

योगाभ्यासबलेनैव नश्येयुः पातकानि तु।

तस्माद्योगपरो भूत्वा ध्यायेन्नित्यं क्रियापरः॥३॥

By virtue of constant practice of *yoga* all the sins are absolved. Therefore in course of performing all religious rites one interested in *yoga* should daily take up meditation.(3)

प्राणायामेन वचनं प्रत्याहारेण चेन्द्रियम्।

धारणाभिर्वशे कृत्वा पूर्वं दुर्धर्षणं मनः॥४॥

एकाकारमना मन्दं बोधरूपमनामयम्।[१]
सूक्ष्मात् सूक्ष्मतरं ध्यायेत् जगदाधारमुच्यते॥५॥

First through *prāṇāyāma* (restraining or suspending the breath during the mental recitation of the names or attributes of a deity) one should control the speech; through *pratyāhāra* (restraining the sense-organs) one controls the sense-organs; through *dhāraṇā* (steady abstraction of mind) one controls the fickle and unsteady mind. Then the person with single-minded devotion should steadily meditate on the (divine) form, the embodiment of consciousness and (bliss), free from all sufferings which is subtler than the subtlest and rightly called the sole support of the universe.(4-5)

आत्मानं बहिरन्तस्थं शुद्धचामीकरप्रभम्।
रहस्येकान्तमासीनो ध्यायेदामरणान्तिकम्॥६॥

The Supreme Self who is inside the heart and outside, resplendent lke the pure gold should be meditated upon till death by one seated in solitude.(6)

यत्सर्वप्राणिहृदयं सर्वेषाञ्च हृदि स्थितम्।
यच्च सर्वजनैर्ज्ञेयं सोऽहमस्मीति चिन्तयेत्॥७॥

The Supreme Self seated in the heart of each and every being, worthy of being known by one and all, represents the heart of all creatures. And during meditation the person should direct his thought process to the effect—"I am identical with the Supreme Self".(7)

आत्मलाभसुखं यावत्तपोध्यानमुदीरितम्।
श्रुतिस्मृत्यादिकं धर्मं तद्विरुद्धं न चाचरेत्॥८॥

Penance and meditation should continue till the bliss of realisation of self is achieved. Till the bliss of self-realisation he should carry on the rites and duties as prescribed by *Śrutis* and *Smṛtis*, but need not act to the contrary.(8)

यथा रथोऽश्वहीनस्तु यथाश्वो रथिहीनकः।
एवं तपश्च विद्या च संयुतं भैषजं भवेत्॥९॥

As the chariot is of no use without the horse; and the horse is useless without a charioteer, so *tapas* and knowledge united together constitute an infallible medicine.(9)

यथान्नं मधुसंयुक्तम् मधुवान्नेन संयुतम्।
उभाभ्यामपि पक्षाभ्यां यथा खे पक्षिणां गतिः॥१०॥
तथैव ज्ञानकर्मभ्यां प्राप्यते ब्रह्म शाश्वतम्।
विद्यातपोभ्यां संपन्नो ब्राह्मणो योगतत्परः॥११॥
देहद्वयं विहायाशु मुक्तो भवति बन्धनात्।
न तथा क्षीणदेहस्य विनाशो विद्यते क्वचित्॥१२॥

As food mixed with honey and honey mixed with food are palatable, and a bird can fly in the sky only with both the wings, through both knowledge and action a man gets the vision of eternal Brahman. A *brāhmaṇa* endowed with knowledge and *tapas*, devoted to the practice of *yoga* immediately casts off the two bodies (the material body and the subtle body) and gets released from the fetters of *saṁsāra*. And after fall of the body (after both the bodies are destroyed) the liberated soul hardly perishes (it is no more subject to decay and death).(10-12)

मया ते[२] कथितः सर्व्वो वर्णाश्रमविभागशः।
संक्षेपेण द्विजश्रेष्ठा! धर्मस्तेषां सनातनः॥१३॥

O revered sages! thus in course of speaking to you of the division of *varṇas* and *āśramas* briefly I have told you everything about the code of conduct fixed for each of these *varṇas* and *āśramas*.(13)

श्रुत्वैवं मुनयो धर्मं स्वर्गमोक्षफलप्रदम्।
प्रणम्य तमृषिं जग्मुर्मुदिताः स्वं स्वमाश्रमम्॥१४॥

Thus the sages listened from Hārīta the account of morality and religion leading to heaven and liberation; they bowed down to that sage and with pleasure repaired to their respective hermitages.(14)

धर्मशास्त्रमिदं सर्वं हारीतमुखनिःसृतम्।
अधीत्य कुरुते धर्मं स याति परमां गतिम्॥१५॥

One who reads the Religious Code as narrated by Hārīta and conducts oneself acc-ordingly, goes to the highest abode.(15)

ब्राह्मणस्य तु यत् कर्म कथितं बाहुजस्य च।
ऊरुजस्यापि यत् कर्म्म कथितं पादजस्य च।
अन्यथा वर्तमानस्यु सद्यः पतत्ति जातितः॥१६॥

The code of conduct in respect of each of the *varṇas*-*brāhmaṇa*, *kṣatriya* (begotten from the arms of the Great

Puruṣa), *vaiśya* (begotten from the thighs) and *śūdra* (begotten from the feet)[3] has been narrated. One who deviates from the prescribed code, is at once, degraded from one's caste.(16)

यो यस्याभिहितो धर्मः स तु तस्य तथैव च।

तस्मात् स्वधर्मं कुर्व्वीत द्विजो नित्यमनापदि॥१७॥

A person is required to abide by the prescribed code of conduct peculiar to his or her *varṇa* and *āśrama*; therefore except in emergency a twice-born should constantly stick to his prescribed duties.(17)

वर्णाश्चत्वारो राजेन्द्र! चत्वारश्चापि चाश्रमाः।

स्वधर्मं ये तु तिष्ठन्ति ते यान्ति परमां गतिम्॥१८॥

O sovereign lord, there are four *varṇas* and four *āśramas*; persons who strictly adhere to the way of life prescribed for their *varṇas* and *āśramas*, attain the highest bliss.(18)

स्वधर्मेण यथा नृणां नारसिंहः प्रसीदति।

न तुष्यति तथान्येन कर्मणा मधुसूदनः॥१९॥

Lord Narsiṁha is pleased with people following their own code of conduct. The Lords, the slayer of the demon Madhu is not so much pleased with any other act as he is pleased with strict adherance to one's own code of conduct.(19)

अतः कुर्वन्निजं कर्म्म यथाकालमतन्द्रितः।

सहस्त्रानीकदेवेशं नारसिंहञ्च सालयम्॥२०॥

Hence without giving oneself to stupor, one doing one's duties in time attains the abode of Narsiṁha, the thousand-rayed Lord of gods.(20)

उत्पन्नवैराग्यबलेन योगी
ध्यायेत्परं ब्रह्म सदा क्रियावान्।
सत्यं सुखं रूपमनन्तमाद्यं
विहाय देहं पदमेति विष्णोः॥२१॥

In course of performing the religious rites a Yogin, by virtue of the spirit of detachment sprung in him, should always meditate on primeval endless Supreme Brahman who is the nature of truth and bliss. Thereafter giving up his body he goes to the abode of Viṣṇu.(21)

इति लघुहारीते-धर्मशास्त्रे सप्तमोऽध्यायः।

इति लघु-हारीत-स्मृतिः समाप्ता।

NOTES

1. The reading बुधैरूपमलामयम् in the *Laghu-Hārīta-Smṛti* of *Aṣṭādaśa-Smṛti, Smṛti-Sandarbha* Part-II, *Dharmaśāstra-Saṁgraha* Vol.I (Jīvānanda), the reading बुधैरूपमनामयम् in the *Laghu-Hārīta-Smṛti* of *Dharmaśāstra-Saṁgraha* (Mahādevā Shastri), *Dharmaśāstra-Saṁgraha* (Vol. I (Upādhayāya) and the reading बुधरूपमनामयम् noticed in the *Hārīta-Saṁhitā* by Dutt make no sense. However, we meet with the correct reading बोधरूपमनामयम् in the *Hārīta-Saṁhitā* appearing in the collection *Unaviṁśati-Saṁhitā* edited by Tarkaratna.

2. Only in the *Laghu-Hārīta-Smṛti* appearing in the *Aṣṭādaśa Smṛti* the reading is च: in place of ते noticed in all other texts.
3. In the famous *Puruṣa sūkta* of *Ṛgveda* (x. 90) we come across the allegorical representation of four *varṇas.* The *brāhmaṇas* are said to have emerged from the mouth of the Great Puruṣa, the *kṣatriyas* from the arms, *vaiśyas* from the thighs and the *śūdras* from the feet.

Bibliography

TEXTS AND TRANSLATION

1. **Saṁhitās, Epics and Purāṇas :**

Ṛgveda-Saṁhitā—Arya Sahitya Mandala Ltd., Ajmer, 1952

The Hymns of the Ṛgveda—(Translation with a popular commentary) Ralph T. H. Griffith, Motilal Banarsidass, Delhi, 1976.

Vājasaneyi-Mādhyandina-Śukla-Yajurveda Saṁhitā—(With the commentaries of Uvaṭa and Mahīdhara) Motilal Banarsidass, Delhi, 1978.

The Texts of the White Yajurveda (Translated with a popular commentry)—Ralph T. H. Griffith, Varanasi, 1976.

Hārīta-Gītā—*The Mahābhārata* (Cr. Edn.) Vol. III, B.O.R.I., Poona, 1974.

The *Brahmāṇḍa Mahāpurāṇam*—by Dr. K. V. Sarma, Krishnadas Academy, Varanasi, 1983.

Narasiṁha Purāṇa—(Text with Hindi Translation), Kalyāṇa Journal, 45th year Nos I & II, Gita Press, Gorakhpur, January-February, 1971.

The Narasiṁha Purāṇa—(Text with English Translation

and Notes) by Dr. S. Jena, Nag Publishers, Delhi, 1987.

Vāyu Purāṇa—Nag Publishers, Delhi, 1983.

The Vāyu Purāṇ—(English Trans.) Part I—G. V. Tagare, Motilal Banarsidass, Delhi, 1987.

2. Smṛti-Texts :

Hārīta-Saṁhitā—(Text with English Translation) by M. N. Dutt, Calcutta, 1906.

Hārīta-Saṁhitā—(Text with Bengali Translation)—Unaviṁśati *Saṁhitā*, Ed. by Pañcānana Tarkaratna, Vaṅgavāsī Press, Calcutta, Baṅgābda 1300.

Laghu-Hārīta-Smṛti–(Containing 117 verses) *Smṛtīnām Samuccayaḥ* Ed. by Hari Narayana Apte, A.S.S., Pune, 1905.

—*Smṛtīnām Samuccayaḥ*-Ed. by Vinayaka Ganesa Apte, A.S.S., Pune, 1929.

Laghu-Hārīta-Smṛti—(Containing 7 Chapters & 194 verses)—*Dharmaśāstra-Saṁgraha* Vol. I Ed. by Jivānanda Vidyāsāgara Bhaṭṭācārya, Calcutta, 1876.

—*Dharmaśāstra-Saṁgraha* or *Aṣṭāviṁśati Smṛtayaḥ*—Mahadeva Shastri, Bombay, Śaka era 1809.

—*Dharmaśāstra-Saṁgraha*, Vol. I, Ed. by Vachaspati Upadhyaya, Navrang, Delhi, 1982.

—*Smṛti Sandarbha* Part II, Manasukharaya Mor, Calcutta, 1957.

—(Text with Hindi Translation) by Pt. Mihir Chand, Nag Publishers, Delhi, 1990.

Śrīvāsiṣṭha-Dharmaśāstram—Rev. Alois Anton Fuhrer, B.O.R.I., Poona, 1930.

Vṛddha-Hārīta-Saṁhitā—(Containing 8 Chapters & about 2600 verses)—*Dharmaśāstra-Saṁgraha* Vol. I, Ed. by Vachaspati Upadhyaya, Navrang, Delhi, 1982.

3. Dictionaries :

Śabdakalpadruma—Vol. V—Raja Radhakanta Deb, Nag Publishers, Delhi, 1987.

V. S. Apte's Practical Sanskrit-English Dictionary—Part II & III Ed. by P. K. Gode and C. G. Karve, Prasad Prakashan, Poona, 1958, 1959.

Secondary Literature

Basham, A. L.—*The Wonder that was India*—Rupa & Co. Delhi, 1988.

Derrett, J. Duncan M.—*Dharmaśāstra and Juridical Literature.* Otto Harrassowitz, Wiesbaden, 1973.

Jena, S.—*The Narasiṁha Purāṇa—A Study,* Nag Publishers, Delhi 1987.

Kane, P. V.—*History of Dharmaśāstra* Vol. I, Part I, B.O.R.I., Poona, 1968.

—*History of Dharmaśāstra* Vol. II, Part I, B.O.R.I., Poona, 1974.

Index of Ślokas in the Text

ह

Index

✦✦✦